COMPANIONS
ALONG
THE
WAY

COMPANIONS ALONG THE WAY

Paul Wilkes

THOMAS MORE PRESS
Chicago, Illinois

The author and publisher are grateful to the following for permission to include copyrighted material:

Thomas Merton: *New Seeds of Contemplation.* Copyright © 1961 by the Abbey of Gethsemani, Inc. Reprinted by permission of New Directions Publishing Corporation.

Thomas Merton: *My Argument with the Gestapo.* Copyright © 1969 by the Abbey of Gethsemani, Inc. Reprinted by permission of New Directions Publishing Corporation.

From MARKINGS by Dag Hammarskjöld, translated by Leif Sjoberg and W. H. Auden. Translation Copyright © 1964 by Alfred A. Knopf, Inc. and Faber and Faber Ltd. Reprinted by permission of Alfred A. Knopf, Inc.

ISBN 0-88347-238-4

Contents

For Tracy, Noah and Daniel

My Companions Along the Way

Acknowledgments

I was fortunate to have two fine libraries available for my research and, more importantly, people within those libraries who greeted me with both expertise and enthusiasm. At the University of Pittsburgh's Hillman Library, Fern Brody and then Laurie Cohen pointed out books and material to me that I would surely have overlooked. At the College of the Holy Cross in Worcester, Massachusetts, James Hogan, the head librarian, readily opened their stacks to me and then guided me through them.

Father Bernard Bonowitz, OCSO, who read through my early draft, has a grasp of history and felicity with the English language that saved me from sins both of commission and omission. He is a Trappist monk at St. Joseph's Abbey in Spencer, Massachusetts. Lawrence Cunningham, professor of religion at the University of Notre Dame, read through many of the profiles and, with his usual intelligence and grace, made them more accurate as well as clearer. Mark Edington, a young though wise man, considerably improved a later version.

And, my thanks go to my friends and acquaintances who told me of the companions who walk with them.

Paul Wilkes

"Only the person who can consciously assent to the power of the inner voice becomes a personality."

Carl Jung

Introduction

We all need to be inspired. Yes, I'm aware that such a word has a slightly warm and moist feeling to it, that echoes of "this is good for you" come rumbling across the landscapes of our individual lives. But it just happens to be true.

Inspiration is as necessary to leading a worthwhile life —not to mention a happy and interesting one—as exercise is to keeping a body functioning. Without exercise, our bodies become weak and eventually, when asked to climb those stairs or lift that carton, cannot perform. If we are not continually (or even occasionally) inspired, our dreams and hopes fade; our souls atrophy.

Throughout the various seasons of our lives, inspiration comes in different forms. Early on, we are inspired by a loving, supportive parent or teacher or by a hero or heroine from worlds as varied as sports and movies or religion and public service. Later we begin to find ourselves mysteriously and wonderfully enheartened by a

9

Introduction

chance acquaintance or a long-time friend, by something read or seen or heard. But as we grow into adulthood and learn more of the capriciousness and unfairness of life, as youthful innocence and idealism are forced to stand up to the test of the real world, of jobs, family, politics—and as we periodically examine the balance sheet of our performance as human beings—inspiration seems harder to find.

To be sure, there are any number of voices calling to us. We hear their promises every day, saying that by following a prescribed ten steps or by believing these tenets or that psychological principle we will be assured of a better life, contentment, can do anything we want, be whomever we wish to be. But, as we learn that such sure-thing, quick fixes don't last, we are equally aware that indeed we are the authors of our lives. What we need is something more: continuing, substantial, meaningful. Philosopher Robert Nozick says it well in his book *The Examined Life:* "An ideal is an image of something higher, and having an ideal, pursuing it, lifts us higher too. We want to have ideals—some ideals, at least—and not simply desires and goals; we want to envision something higher and seek it."

Companions Along the Way is one man's attempt to supply inspiration in his own life. It is based on a simple enough premise: that through knowledge of the lives of those who have fought the good fight, yearned to be good and do right, a person will be infused with the means to live a better life.

While we constantly hear that ours is an especially amoral, hedonistic, godless, selfish time, any cursory reading of history reveals that such wails of condemnation have gone up many, many times before. Perhaps the vision of goodness and greatness seems unduly blurred today, but men and women have always sought ways to shape their lives and measure their behavior. In the pages that follow, twenty people are presented who might be of help.

But beware: these Companions are an odd lot. They do not espouse a special "way." They neither adhere to a uniform doctrine nor are they members of any one faith. Some in essence "lost" their faith, some found it; one of them was a pagan. Many of their names you already know, but you may not know them from this perspective, which focuses on the moral, spiritual, religious or transcendent power coursing through their lives.

What links the Companions is that each felt and responded to a certain moral vision or ethical imperative, a force that caused them to act as they did. While they were constantly confronted with their own frailty and shortcomings, they were absolutely driven by the insatiable hunger to find and live the inner meaning of life. They boldly confronted the difficult moral issues of their day—and daily wrestled with them.

We might say that they had some sort of inner compass that helped them steer their course. A phrase that is often linked to one of the Companions, Flannery O'Connor, seems to sum it up in a plainspoken way—they had a "habit of being." This "habit of being," Sally Fitzgerald wrote of her good friend O'Connor, was "an excellence not only of action but of interior disposition . . . and was itself reflected in what she did and said." So it is a quality of mind, or as Jacques Maritain, O'Connor's

Introduction

inspiration said, "a virtue of the practical intellect." It is not a quality implanted at birth, but one schooled and tempered throughout life.

The Companions come from varied walks of life, cultures and countries. While some were most visible, like Thomas More and Marcus Aurelius, others lived at the margins: Charles de Foucauld in the desert, George Herbert in a tiny rural parish. Some are towering intellectuals—Spinoza, Aldous Huxley and Ralph Waldo Emerson—while Harriet Tubman and Akiba were illiterate for much of their lives. Some turned their back on the religion of their youth and others embraced it. Many had an enormously difficult time finding their way and some had quite unlikely early years—de Foucauld was a libertine soldier, Thomas Merton a roustabout college student, Jane Addams and Edith Stein fought deep depression, Dag Hammarskjöld outwardly successful but internally dead.

If the reader is looking for consistency in these people, they will disappoint you. They were hardly saintly or pious. Their lives were not one smooth, inexorable movement toward goodness. Many of the Companions failed horribly even after they had once measured up heroically to needs of the moment. And when they did succeed in finally leading what would be considered worthwhile lives, they were not always applauded. Within the period of a few years, Jane Addams was called both one of the most admired women in America and one of the most dangerous. Hammarskjöld was praised as a peacemaker and condemned as lackey. Thomas More, once one of the most powerful men in English government, was beheaded. Spinoza's commu-

Introduction

nity in Amsterdam thought him mad; and when Herbert turned his back on a budding career in Parliament, friends abandoned him.

Yet, regardless of personal setbacks and the ebb and flow of public opinion, they went on, toward goals that appeared unreachable, with visions that often seemed absurd, with principles considered misguided and foolish. They fell often, but they never ultimately succumbed to the seductive call of currently acceptable morality. They dramatize that in every age, in strange and wonderfully diverse ways, goodness and morality are afoot.

Although the Companions may have thought of themselves as failures, history shows they emerged victorious. And knowing this, we can feel buttressed in our individual lives, quickened by people who have thoughtfully gone down other paths, or who have faced problems and issues strikingly similar to our own. And knowing these Companions, we can go on ourselves, not with our heads hung low, our jaws clenched, but instead refreshed after this contact with their power.

What struck me over and over as I learned more about the Companions was that in their struggle to discover what they should give their life to, and then how to conduct that life, they were often seeking out a self they had earlier bypassed. The basically good and decent instincts of their youth somehow had been displaced and until they had righted themselves, they could have no peace.

Perhaps this rings true for many people—where is that me I once was? Where is the clear vision of life I

Introduction

once had? Why am I acting as I am now? I would have never tolerated such a person as I now am had I come in contact with him or her five or ten or thirty or fifty years ago. I have my worldly accomplishments, but when they are stripped away, what is left of me?

What *Companions Along the Way* may do is to reacquaint you with that self which may have been displaced. A self you want to regain. A side of you that should not be allowed to wither, but should be helped to thrive. Hopefully, it is a book that not only offers inspiration, but encouragement and insight as well.

Companions might be used in a number of ways.

1) To be read and enjoyed—after all, these are fascinating people—and beyond that, perhaps to provide the inspiration required in the circumstances of your life.

2) As a starting point for an informal group or a class. Life stories—biographical or autobiographical—provide a means for looking at our own. In these lives, we can see bits of ourselves—at our best, at our worst.

3) As source material for adults who are undergoing religious education or are about to join a church or synagogue.

4) As an introduction and an invitation to learn more about any of the Companions who speak especially to you. A selected list of books by or about each Companion follows his or her chapter.

5) For family members to read and talk over.

But, please, do not treat *Companions* as a study guide, as required, "good for you" reading. Sufficient biographical and historical background are given so that

Introduction

the fabric and development of each character is in clear relief, but there are no questions or discussion topics at the end of each chapter. Rather, consider *Companions Along the Way* as an opportunity to spend a little time with some wonderful people, people who have something to say to you today. There is the freshness of a new acquaintance, combined with the certitude of enduring greatness.

Read, and let your mind go where it will.

I. Lifting
a Yoke

Akiba

Albert Schweitzer

Spinoza

Harriet Tubman

Akiba

The late bloomers among us will find solace in the life of Akiba, the legendary Jewish sage. Perseverance, common sense and a great sense of humor stood him well in a life that started so humbly and ended in greatness. If Flannery O'Connor had a "habit of being," Akiba surely had a "habit of mind."

A WANDERING tribe—in many ways like other wandering tribes at the beginning of the 2nd millenium before Christ—made a pact with what they came to know as God. They would accept and honor Him and in return, He would grant them protection and prosperity. Through centuries of paganism and idol worship as the common form of acknowledgment of a higher power, the Israelites struggled to understand not only what their covenant meant, but how best to keep it.

Abraham based the pact on a set of simple, terse commands from God, which were later elaborated upon and became the Torah, the first five books of the Bible. Jacob renewed the pact with God and Moses affirmed and restated this intimate relationship when he came down from Mt. Sinai to confront his faithless, frightened people. Jewish law grew through the centuries, inspired by God, but constantly tempered and formed by man as reason was brought to bear on the eternal religious questions as well as the dilemmas of the day. A living body of communal law—both written and oral—was developed that set the Jews apart, assured their survival and ingeniously provided a vast framework for everything from worship to hygiene.

But as with any code, Jewish law at times became an end in itself, rather than a means to reach toward God. Rituals, intended to assure unity, instead become burdens. The keepers of the law made it a yoke rather than a bridge, demanding complicated observances, sacrifices and offerings the poor couldn't afford.

Such a time in Jewish history occurred during the 1st and into the 2nd century A.D. Within some hundred years, tiny Palestine gave birth to rabbinical Judaism and to Christianity. Jerusalem, at one time the hub of a prosperous Jewish empire, was destroyed, the great temple demolished; her people were slaughtered, sold into slavery or forced to flee to other lands. It was a time when Rome alternately condoned and crushed the Jews and when Jews fought among themselves, factionalism tearing at the very fabric of their society. In those days, patrician, land-owning Jews expected the strict observance of the Law from the huge numbers of landless peasant Jews, artisans and tradesmen who had been driven from Jerusalem and were trying to eke out an existence, while keeping their faith.

A man for this season emerged and, enveloped in a wonderful swirl of legend and truth, mysticism and rationality, comes down to the present day to advise us on our life's journey. His name was Akiba and he had that rare combination of traits: wisdom and divinely-directed—but humanly-rooted—common sense.

Perhaps it's best to first acknowledge the person really responsible for his transformation from an illiterate shepherd to a Talmudic sage: the good woman Rachel. Rachel, the daughter of Akiba's employer, one of the wealthiest Jews in Judea, somehow saw through his coarse, rough exterior. He was an *am ha-arez*, lower-class, illiterate, landless, already an older man, with no future except a life of labor. He lived in a hut made of dried clay and slept on a straw mat on the bare floor. Rachel had been raised in a mansion, with servants looking after her needs. But she wanted to marry him anyhow, extracting a promise that he would devote his life to the study of the Torah. To Rachel and other observant Jews, there was nothing higher than the study of the law; it was the highest form of worship, an expression of love for God. Her father was not as impressed with her choice of a partner and cut them off; and though Rachel at one time had to sell her hair for food, she kept her promise, as Akiba did his.

Akiba was a contemporary of St. Paul and like Paul he held in utter disgust the very group he would eventually join—Paul, the Christians, Akiba, the rabbinical scholars. But unlike Paul, who after his conversion would set about preaching the Good News, Akiba first had to lay a foundation for what would become his work. He went to school with his five-year-old son and, seated alongside him, learned the alphabet, then reading and writing. Akiba was not a natural student and many times, frustrated with his inability to grasp the material, was ready to return to his sheep and goats. When finally he was able to read Hebrew texts, he was given not the wonderful story of Genesis, but—as was the custom in his day—the incredibly technical laws of sacrifice contained in Leviticus. Mind-numbing regulations for burnt offerings and sin offerings, the detailing of various sexual and skin diseases had to be mastered. What sacrifices were to be performed in what part of the temple, with what animals; what kind of pottery was to be used; water from what source.

Akiba wanted to get back to the pasture.

But there was Rachel behind him and, although he didn't know it, before him an illustrious career and a place in history as a man who humanized divine law.

At the age of 40, this balding peasant went to the prestigious institute at Yabneh where the sons of the wealthy as well as wild-eyed fanatics studied the ancient scriptures and the oral traditions of Judaism and wrestled to apply the ancient teachings to their everyday life. The outdoor lessons and debates were far more than a course of study—they were the Jews' entertainment, sport, pastime, pleasure and passion. Faced with a world that largely misunderstood them and often turned violent toward them, the Jews of antiquity entered daily into the world of biblical and talmudic learning for solace and perspective.

Akiba

Initially Akiba was undistinguished, another face in the crowd. But what he had brought with him—his age and his experiences—eventually proved immeasurably helpful. He came to the law as a middle-aged man and could approach it with fresh vision, understanding its glories as well as its shortcomings. He had seen the rich and powerful profit by the law, while poor families like his own suffered under rigid rules. Slowly, he began to speak out and, calling upon his unique background—as enhanced by his fertile intellect—he became known for his wisdom.

According to accepted rabbinic law, seeds that Jewish priests received as an offering but which were not used immediately could be planted—but as the seeds kept their sacredness, whatever grew from them could only be eaten by the priests. Only poor priests were allowed to go into the fields to glean what remained after the harvest. This struck Akiba as totally unfair and he argued that the rights of the vast number of the poor—who were customarily allowed to glean—were being denied. His answer: allow the poor to glean and then to sell what they had gathered to the priests.

Ancient Jewish tradition forbade women to adorn themselves with makeup or perfume or fine clothes during their menstrual period, when they were considered impure and unclean. Akiba presciently argued that this could only lead to loss of marital love and in the process revamped the whole conception of the relationship between husband and wife. He forwarded the then revolutionary thought that a wife must not only be beautiful and presentable when she was fertile, but even when she could not conceive. Akiba was trying to impress upon his people that love, not sex, needed to be the basis of marriage.

He was a champion of the downtrodden and the poor and was forever exhorting the Jews to generosity, often quoting from the Book of Proverbs, "Charity delivereth from death." He was also a great story-teller, his home-spun parables illustrating basic religious themes.

Soothsayers warned his daughter that on her wedding night she would be bitten by a serpent, one of Akiba's stories began. She was taking off her clothes after the wedding celebration—the dire prediction forgotten in her happiness—when she threw a pin into a hole in the wall. She withdrew it the next morning to find she had killed a serpent. When Akiba asked her to explain this miracle, she remembered that a poor man had come to the gate while the wedding guests were eating. No one would have anything to do with him, but she took pity on him and gave him one of her costly gifts. Charity triumphed in many of Akiba's tales.

Hundreds of Akiba's wise pronouncements are woven into the tapestry of Jewish thought. "The attraction of sin is first as feeble as a spider's thread, but ultimately it becomes as strong as a ship's cable." When asked how Jews should act toward this new splinter group, the Christians, he quoted what he felt was the basic princi-ple of the Torah, "Love thy neighbor as thyself."

His opinions were sought on a wide range of issues, but Akiba's religion was certainly much more than an intellectual pursuit. Underlying everything he learned and taught was an abiding faith in God, childlike in its innocence and depth. "Whatever God does is for the best," he constantly admonished those who bemoaned what misfortunes had been visited upon them. He told a story of visiting a town where there was no guesthouse, which forced Akiba and two companions to sleep in the field. Naturally, they felt put out by the inconvenience. With them they had an ass, a rooster and a flame. During the night, a lion killed the ass, a cat killed the rooster; and wind extinguished the flame. During that same night a band of Bedouins attacked the city and took all the inhabitants captive. Had he and his companions been in the city, had the animals made any noise or the flame burned brightly, they would have suffered a similar fate.

Equally endearing about this giant of Jewish life is his humility. He and Eliezer, the renowned leader of the academy, were constantly at odds over their differing interpretations of the law. Once, during a severe drought, Eliezer was asked to lead the people in prayer to relieve the drought. Nothing happened. A few days later, Akiba lead the prayers; he had hardly begun when the rains fell. It would have been so easy to smile smugly or bow his head in false acquiesence as the people congratulated him, but instead, Akiba turned the event to his master's favor. He told a story of a king who had two daughters, one lovable, the other repulsive. When the lovable daughter came to him with a request, the king would never grant it immediately, preferring to hear her voice, to have her with him. The other daughter immediately got what she wanted, so he could be rid of her.

The amazing thing about Akiba is that, in his own mind, he was not introducing anything new into Judaism. His principles were basic: worship was paramount, superstition forbidden; the poor and women and slaves must be uplifted, priests must be honored, but their power limited. He saw himself merely as a conduit, the connector between the Torah and the Chosen People, trying to make the Law clear and just. As a trial would open and the litigants would come before him, Akiba would say, "Know before whom ye are standing." They knew the great man of course; but then Akiba would add, "Not before Akiba ben Joseph, but before the Holy One, Blessed be He."

Had Akiba done no more than be a wise and fair judge, he would still be revered today; but after 15 years at the academy, when he was around 55, he began the exhaustive compilation of Jewish law. Before his time, laws were collected not under logical headings, but by the similarity of their literary formulation. Festival observances, legal norms for proper punishments, or the form for prayers might all be gathered in one melodic but confusing statement. It was a beautiful idea, but a nightmare for anyone searching for juridical continuity or precedent or for those trying to clarify theological thought.

In codifying the *Mishnah,* Akiba not only sorted, but boldly changed the law. He brought to bear a precise but example-studded style that students found easier to remember, for the *Mishnah* had to be committed to memory. As importantly, he took the laws and traditions and linked them to the biblical verses on which they were based. In Akiba's lifetime, his *Mishnah* was enormously popular; in later years, scholars of the Talmud would say that Akiba had virtually saved the Torah from oblivion. Not only Jews, but Christian church fathers referred to him as a second Moses.

What Akiba accomplished is truly mind-boggling: he had, in essence, compiled a philosophy combining ethics, natural and divine law, religion, theology and politics. Jewish law, in Akiba's hands, became so comprehensive that, to draw a parallel, it was as though natural law, the Bible, canon law, English common law, parliamentary statutes, the American Constitution and the Charter of the United Nations had been brought together in one place.

Late in life, in his 70s, Akiba was called upon to fill yet another role, the one for which he is perhaps most famous: statesman. Rome's promise to rebuild the Temple in Jerusalem had been cavalierly retracted, giving rise to a new nationalist movement whose proponents vowed to take back their holy city at any cost and re-establish the place of worship central to their religious observances. Unbelievable carnage and destruction ensued; entire communities were massacred; Jews were deported; brides were carried off on the night before their weddings.

When there was not open warfare, there were periods of insidious repression as Rome sought to eradicate these troublesome Jews from its empire. Circumcision, the sounding of the *shofar,* and scores of the public religious services at the heart of Judaism were banned. Jewish courts were throttled. Ardent extremists were understandably incensed. To them, only constant rebellion would overcome this oppression. The Messiah was at hand, awaiting their call, they were sure. They would hasten His arrival by fighting the enemies of Judaism at every turn.

Akiba counseled patience. He was soundly denounced as an irresolute weakling.

This man who had given his life to the proper observance of Jewish ritual, who time and again called it the key to the survival of his people, now seemed to be accommodating the hated Romans. His opponents were ready to die for this cause; it was a time to stand fast on their beliefs. Was their obeisance to God's law or Caesar's?

Akiba, who so often would not hear of compromise when it came to the observances of his religion, did not see this latest move by Rome in such terms. While such prohibitions were repugnant to him, Akiba advised observing the Law in private and continuing the study of the Torah. Rome would pass away; the Law would never die. The intellect was powerful; violence was self-defeating.

As had so many earthly powers before, Rome found it could neither annihilate these steadfast people nor legislate them out of existence. Finally the study of the Torah itself was outlawed. There could be no compromise here for Akiba and he continued to teach. He was now 90 and his friends warned that he was courting death, to which Akiba replied with a story about the fox who invited the fish to come onto the bank rather than risk being caught by fishermen. The fish replied, "If in the water, which is our element, we are in danger, what will happen to us on the dry land, which is not our element?" Even after he was imprisoned, Akiba's wisdom was still sought; disciples would come to his cell window

Akiba

with their difficult questions and Akiba would shout down his guidance.

For violating the ban on the Torah, Akiba was sentenced to death. The Romans killed him by tearing his flesh from his living body with hooks. In unspeakable agony, Akiba called out in words forbidden by his earthly masters, but sweet to the ear of the One above:

"Hear, O Israel, the Lord is our God, the Lord is One. And thou shalt love the Lord thy God with all thine heart, and with all thy soul, and with all thy might."

The Roman general overseeing this gruesome execution could not believe what he was seeing and hearing. Was it magic or could this man not feel pain?

"I have always loved the Lord with all my might, and with all my heart," Akiba uttered. "Now I know that I love him with all my life."

Akiba is a favorite among rabbinical students and religious Jews, but he is hardly known beyond those circles. What a pity. For not only is his imprint on virtually every page of the Talmud, his sense of justice is embodied in many documents that nations and religions have formulated in the centuries since his death. He believed the law should lead to human happiness, a simple yet universal mandate that he carried out so well.

Finkelstein, Louis, *Akiba: Scholar, Saint and Martyr,* Atheneum (Temple Book), New York, 1970.

Albert Schweitzer

*It takes a strong-willed
person to be good, no doubt
of that; but the life of Albert
Schweitzer shows that even
while doing good, a person
can be harshly criticized.
Don't expect applause for
what you are doing—you
might be ridiculed instead.
But something deep inside
will keep reminding you to
go on, pursuing your
individual vision of leading a
worthwhile life.*

THE YEAR was 1913 and the handsome Alsatian
with a full head of thick, curly dark hair presented
himself before the Paris Missionary Society and offered
his services. He mentioned nothing of how his family and
friends had discouraged him. They had told him he was
throwing away his life; his prodigious talents would be

wasted among the savages in the tropical wasteland where he wanted to go.

He indeed had an impressive dossier: an accomplished organist and composer, he held degrees in music, theology, philosophy and medicine. He was already considered an expert on Bach and had published well-acclaimed books in music, religion and ethics.

But the members of the missionary board were not awed by his credentials. They were more concerned about his orthodoxy. Would this Albert Schweitzer who had come before them retell the Bible stories truthfully or with some radical new interpretation? Could he be relied upon to uphold the mainstream Protestant view of religion? After all, this Dr. Schweitzer had had the audacity to take on no less a subject for his doctorate in medicine than Jesus Christ Himself—and a psychiatric appraisal at that! This, following upon his book *The Quest of the Historical Jesus,* was hardly the sign of a readily compliant soul. And at 38, he was older than most applicants. Was he going toward something, or merely running away? Could he be entrusted with the care of souls?

All the doctor could say in his own defense was what he firmly believed: that desire to serve people—not theological orthodoxy—should be the determining factor in their decision to send him to the remote outpost in French Equatorial Africa to start a hospital. But, if lack of orthodoxy was their concern, he vowed he would practice medicine and not religion.

While Albert Schweitzer ultimately practiced medicine and *lived* religion, it is a pity that in the twenty-odd years since his death we have lost sight of what motivated him to do what he did, and how vehemently he was criticized for the way he did it. With that bushy white mustache, characteristic pith helmet, bow tie and sad, droopy eyes, Schweitzer has unfortunately become an icon, conveniently beyond the reach of normal mortals.

But to put his picture on the wall with a candle burning in homage before it would do a great disservice to the man. His life and nature were far too complex and stormy for such deification. It's comfortable to recall he won a Nobel Prize for peace but disconcerting to remember what others said of him: "This proud and obstinate old man has become a tragic anachronism." He saved countless lives in Africa, only to hear "Jungle doctor, go home!" He had unbelievable patience and was prone to unpredictable anger. But above all, he had a vision which he stubbornly kept, regardless of the praise or scorn accorded him. Albert Schweitzer is a living companion, not an inaccessible idol to be blindly honored.

Schweitzer was born in 1875 in the province of Alsace-Lorraine, near the border between France and Germany, which required him to know two languages and immediately cast him as an international man rather than one who owed his allegiance to a single country. His father was a poor, liberal Protestant minister, never too successful, something of a Bohemian and free-thinker.

Schweitzer could point to three events in his youth that shaped him. The first was a bird hunt. Slingshot in hand, he joined the other boys on an outing; but when the moment to shoot came, Albert couldn't let the stone fly. He shooed the birds away instead. The thought of needlessly taking a life—even that of just one of the myriad birds in the countryside—revolted him. Then there was the afternoon when the Jewish peddler drove his cart into town and Albert joined the other boys, running alongside the man, taunting him by shouting his name: "Mausche! Mausche!" The man did nothing in return but trudge on, embarrassed but calm in the face of verbal assault. "From Mausche I learned what it meant to keep silent under persecution, and this was a most valuable lesson," Schweitzer would later write in *Memoirs of Childhood and Youth*. The third event took place in the seaport town of Colmar when Schweitzer, walking about the town, came upon a huge statue "The Suffering African," a rendering of a majestic yet sad slave. It touched something deep within him.

A respect for life. The ability to withstand persecution. An affinity for the people of Africa. All would come together in Schweitzer's life. In time.

He was fascinated by music and extraordinarily talented, even as a child. His deciphering of Bach orchestrations was considered a milestone in classical music, making possible the use of modern instruments to play the master's compositions. And, the study of religion engrossed him, as well. Schweitzer earned doctorates in theology, philosophy and music—anticipating an academic career—and was eventually appointed dean of the Theological College at Strasbourg. He was thrilled with giving lectures and concerts, with writing books, but there was a void in his life that could not be filled.

And there was something else equally troubling to him —far more concrete and immediate. Early in life, he had begun to question the beliefs of his religion and had veered off the well-trod path of traditional Christianity. How could he teach what he did not believe?

Companions Along the Way

The deeper he delved into the historical underpinnings of his faith, the more he saw how the basic message of Christ had been obscured over the centuries. He saw how dogma came to dominate the minds of the faithful and adherence to creeds and attendance at rituals came to embody what it meant to be a practicing Christian. He could shrewdly debate the various interpretations of Paul's Epistles, the meaning of the Last Supper and whatever theological issue was put before him; but his well-reasoned arguments only seemed to take him further away from the essence of Christianity. The virgin birth, resurrection, the deity of Christ, prayer, the supremacy of faith over reason—Schweitzer could not accept many of the venerable tenets of Christianity. Truth, he kept saying—however new, unexpected or at odds with scholarly findings and tradition—could only enhance faith, never damage it.

When he read an article about the pressing need for doctors in West Africa, Schweitzer saw a way. "I wanted to be a doctor that I might be able to work without having to talk," he wrote. "For years I had been giving myself out in words . . . but this new form of activity I could not represent to myself as talking about the religion of love, but only as an actual putting it into practice. . . . I would make my life my argument. I would advocate the things I believed in terms of the life I lived and what I did. Instead of preaching my belief in the existence of God within each of us, I would attempt to let my life and work say what I believed."

Even as Schweitzer was about to turn his back on his successful careers, he remained clear-eyed about what had happened to cause such a profound change. He was not doing it because he had "heard the voice of God." There was no thunder, no parting of the clouds. Some theologians might have had direct communications with God, but Schweitzer admitted he was not one of them. They perhaps had sharper ears, he allowed. No, it was only a simple, quite logical decision, consistent with what he believed: that when a need about which an individual could do something presented itself, it was exactly what the person should do.

The missionary society finally approved him and Schweitzer reached the outpost of Lambarene, on the Ogowe River, in what is now Gabon, ready to go to work. He was shocked by what he found. It was far more primitive than he had imagined and neither the missionary who was supposed to have made arrangements for him nor the orderly who was to assist him were there. He cleaned up the most suitable structure, a hen house, and began to see patients.

Schweitzer had been trained in tropical medicine at the Sorbonne and while he didn't hope to found a modern hospital in the middle of the jungle, he began to offer some basic amenities: beds and sheets, for instance, and meals prepared by his wife, Helene. But, day after day, the food went uneaten. He found that the natives believed that most sicknesses were caused by poisons mixed in the food, and that the most dangerous of such poisons were evil thoughts and wishes. They only trusted food prepared by their own relatives. Schweitzer quickly changed his style.

Visitors to the hospital over the years were often appalled by the seeming chaos and unsanitary conditions at Lambarene. There was no running water. Campfires burned in the courtyards as family members cooked for the patients. They fished in the river for food and went into the jungle to relieve themselves. Whatever laundry there was to do (many patients never used a bed, but recuperated on the floor of one of the huts) was washed out in the river. Animals roamed at will. The stench was overwhelming. To Schweitzer, it was exactly right—not a hospital at all, but a native village in which there happened to be a clinic. A half-century before modern medicine acknowledged how crucial a patient's emotional security was, Schweitzer sensed its importance and ran his hospital to suit the jungle people who came to him. The natives trusted Schweitzer and flocked to Lambarene.

There was no electricity except for the operating room lights and x-ray machine. Medicines were stored wherever it was coolest, often beneath the floor; there was no refrigeration. No motor vehicles were allowed in the compound. When a shipment arrived by boat, Schweitzer would go down to river's edge and help carry the supplies. He not only designed the buildings, but worked on them, hauling logs and weaving palm fronds. He might operate all morning and push a wheelbarrow in the afternoon.

The fame of Albert Schweitzer grew over the years. And so did the hospital complex; eventually it contained some 70 buildings. But Schweitzer changed little.

He once wrote to students of a nursing school: "You ask me to give you a motto. Here it is: SERVICE. Let this word accompany each of you throughout your life. Let it be before you as you seek your way and your duty in the world. May it be recalled to your minds if ever you are tempted to forget it or to set it aside. It will not always be a comfortable companion but it will always be a faithful one. And it will be able to lead you to happiness, no matter what the experiences of your lives are. Never have this word on your lips, but keep it in your hearts. And may it be a confidant that will teach you not only to do good but to do it simply and humbly.''

Schweitzer was a magnificent inspirational thinker and writer; so when visitors came to Lambarene, they invariably expected to see a saintly man in whites, without the stains that mar the rest of mankind, healing with a gentle hand and word. Many went away saddened, not only by the uncleanliness and seeming inefficiency of the place, but by Schweitzer himself, who often talked to the natives as if they were children. He appeared to symbolize the white man's arrogance in a black Africa that was beginning to break the chains of colonialism.

But those who stayed longer got to see that a gruff, sometimes patronizing exterior was certainly not all there was to Schweitzer. He was a man fighting the jungle and disease and lethargy. It took more than patience and kindliness; it took steadfast determination, grit. Some called him patriarchal, a despot. To this Schweitzer once replied, ''An enlightened despot is able to give the greatest amount of freedom.''

His ''reverence for life'' was so profound that no animal in the hospital village was ever killed for food. A bee that found its way into the operating room was caught and released outside. Schweitzer ordered that an orange tree be left standing in the middle of a roadway, rather than have it chopped down for convenience's sake. His staff members urged him to turn away an in-

Companions Along the Way

jured man who had previously stolen drugs from the hospital and sold them in the village. "Whatsoever you do unto the least of these my brethren, you have done it to me," he replied. "This is my image of the Kingdom of God . . . Quick, waste no time. Get him to the operating room."

Thomas Merton had a favorite saying which certainly applies to Schweitzer: "The saint preaches sermons by the way he stands, the way he picks up things and holds them in his hands." Norman Cousins, a visitor to Lambarene in the late 1950s, recalls his horror after dinner as Schweitzer approached an old piano and announced the number of the hymn that would be sung that evening. The jungle had taken its toll on the piano: the keys were stained, screws held the ivory veneer on the keys in place; strings were missing on at least a dozen notes, the sustaining pedal was permanently stuck. "Here was one of history's great interpreters of Bach, a man who could fill any concert hall in the world," Cousins wrote. "I felt not only pain but a certain inspiration in the image of Schweitzer at the old piano. For the amazing and wonderous thing was that the piano seemed to lose its poverty in his hands. Whatever its capacity was to yield music was being fully realized. The tinniness and chattering echoes seemed subdued . . . his being at the piano strangely seemed to make it right."

Some within the medical community, even those who once congratulated him, grew impatient as Schweitzer held on to the practices of his earliest days. His hospital was internationally known; money poured in and the finest specialists came to work with him. But Schweitzer still held the line on electrification, intent on keeping the

38

Albert Schweitzer

village feeling. It was "scandalous," medical professionals pronounced. Yet when a team of researchers did a study of post-operative recovery of Schweitzer's patients, they found the rate better than that of most modern hospitals. And a good number of the cases involved major surgery on people who had had little or no previous medical attention.

Again, at the hands of Albert Schweitzer and those who came to work with him, the ill had been strangely made right. Over 100,000 people were treated at Lambarene.

Schweitzer was offered many honors in his lifetime, but he rarely traveled to be praised—and, equally, he rarely responded to his detractors. He was denounced for denying so many doctrines—he no longer should be called a Christian, some said; he was labeled a "communist dupe" for his opposition to nuclear weapons.

In response, he made a confession. "I must forgive lies directed against me because so many times my own conduct has been blotted by lies, I must forgive the lovelessness, the hatred, the slander, the fraud, the arrogance I encounter, since I myself have so often lacked love, and have hated, slandered, defrauded, and been arrogant, and I must forgive without noise or fuss. In general, I do not succeed in forgiving fully; I do not even get as far as being always just. But he who tries to live by this principle, simple and hard as it is, will know the real adventures and triumphs of the soul."

As Norman Cousins left Lambarene, he tried, like many visitors before him, to sort out exactly what he felt, what he had witnessed. Cousins wrote: "The biggest impression of Albert Schweitzer that emerged was

39

of a man who had learned to use himself fully. Much of the ache and brooding unhappiness in modern life is the result of man's difficulty in using himself fully." Schweitzer ". . . was not concerned about the attainability of perfection; he was concerned about the pursuit of perfection." Cousins concluded, ". . . at Lambarene I learned that a man does not have to be an angel to be a saint."

Many people wrote Schweitzer for advice about their own life's journey. Many said they were ready to come to Lambarene to work with him. Four words of his could serve as a response to the letter people might compose in their heart right now about what direction they should take in their life:

"Everyone has his Lambarene."

Anderson, Erica, *The Schweitzer Album,* Harper & Row, New York, 1965.

Cousins, Norman, *Dr. Schweitzer of Lambarene,* Adam & Charles Black, London, 1960.

Joy, Charles R., ed., *Albert Schweitzer, An Anthology,* Harper & Row, New York, 1965.

Schweitzer, Albert, *Out of My Life and Thought,* New American Library Mentor Book, New York, 1953.

Seaver, George, *Albert Schweitzer, The Man and His Mind,* Harper and Brothers, New York, 1947.

Spinoza

Somehow we know when what is passing for the truth is not true. But what to do when "everyone believes. . ."? Spinoza could not go along with the prevailing beliefs of his time, and so he went off in his own direction. Castigated in his lifetime, he is uniformly praised today.

THEY WERE called Marranos—which literally translated meant "damned ones" or "swine." These Jews who had been forcibly converted to Christianity during the Spanish Inquisition found that, even after they acceded to the Church's wishes, they continued to offend—this time not by their religion but by their success. The Church viewed them as nominal Christians at best, and their rise to positions of power and influence in Spain was yet another troubling (and humiliating) reminder of their inner resources. The only way to deal with them was banishment.

41

Companions Along the Way

A group of exiled Marranos settled in Amsterdam near the end of the 16th century. The Netherlands had declared its independence from Spain and while the political strength of Dutch Calvinists tempered true religious freedom, the Spanish Jews enjoyed a freedom to live, work and worship that many had never experienced.

This was an incredibly stimulating and productive period in Amsterdam. The Dutch West and East India companies were being formed, and with them came international trading and commerce on an unprecedented scale that involved many Jews.

The Jewish community in Amsterdam was unique in many ways. Because of its enormous range of economic interests it was virtually its own nation, negotiating with other countries and cities. It was closely knit, as commerce and the religious beliefs that were now allowed to flourish forged a community that was strong within and a fortress without. It was politically and religiously conservative. Heresy could not be tolerated; the Jews were well aware it was their religion that had ultimately kept them bound together through years of persecution.

Because the Netherlands was not a religious state, it was an equally fertile time for the new intellectual movement that was sweeping across Europe. Galileo and Newton had revolutionized the way man looked at the world he lived in. Descartes, who had lived in Holland, along with Hobbes and Bacon had radically altered man's perception of himself.

One Baruch de Spinoza was born into the Amsterdam Jewish community in 1632, the son of a prosperous merchant. His education was like that of all Jewish boys of Amsterdam, a prescribed curriculum that included the study of the Hebrew Bible, the Talmud and the great medieval Jewish philosophers such as Maimonides. On a parallel track, he was being introduced into his father's business. Someday it would be his.

For most boys, the school in Amsterdam accomplished its intended goal, steeping them in their religion and readying them for a life as observant Jews. For Baruch, it had the opposite effect.

While the words of the Bible were taught to be the literal words of God, young Baruch could not abide by that. The wonderful tales of Scripture enchanted him, but could they be true? In the world around him, a new understanding of nature, undergirded by the precision of mathematics, seemed at odds with the reverential and unquestioning acceptance of the God of his people.

Spinoza went on to study with an ex-Jesuit, Francis Van Den Ende. Through him the young Spinoza was not only exposed to Latin and the sciences, but to Descartes and what was heralded and condemned as "free thinking." Before this time, the world had been considered a finite, ordered whole, a cosmos in which the earth was the center and unchanging heavenly bodies revolved around it. Created substances fell into certain natural categories, each with its unique set of laws.

In the 17th century, physical and philosophical discovery was pointing to a universe different in almost every important way. It was infinite, not finite, ordered not by various laws, but governed by a universal set of laws that could be expressed and explained in mathematical terms. Descartes, a scientist and a Christian, had shaken the very pillars of religious belief by uncompromisingly stating that mind and body were indeed two separate substances which, while intricately linked, needed to be regarded as discrete.

The new rationalism was waging a war against conventional medieval theology.

While he had no desire to give up his faith or his God, Spinoza came to what would have to be considered a terrifying conclusion for a believer of his time: that truth could not be found in dogma. It was clear to him that God was more than words in Scripture; God was not some force outside the world, but was actually within it. Spinoza knew that he had to pursue a truth which was at once elusive yet palpable to him. "I permit each person to live in his own way and, if he so desires, to die for his presumed salvation, if only I may be permitted to live for truth," he would later declare.

The young Spinoza was not only a scandal to the Jews of Amsterdam, he was a threat. His heretical views were attracting the young people of the community and the elders declared that this must stop. He was called before the council of rabbis to answer charges that he was undermining the authority of the scriptures and questioning the Jews' role as the Chosen People. His excommunication from the synagogue marked a turning point in his life.

For this was no simple matter of being barred from the synagogue; it meant total banishment. The community was ready to accept him back, if he would only mend his ways; otherwise he was to be shunned. In the words of the excommunication: "Cursed shall he be in the daytime, and cursed also by night! Cursed shall he be when he lieth down, and cursed when he riseth up! . . . May the Lord not forgive his sins! . . ."

Spinoza

Spinoza, who could not compromise the independence of his thought, was given a frightful freedom —and yet he could say:

> . . . I gladly enter on the path that is opened to me, with the consolation that my departure will be more innocent than was the exodus of the early Hebrews from Egypt. Although my subsistence is no better secured than was theirs, I take away nothing from anybody, and whatever injustice may be done to me, I can boast that people have nothing to reproach me with.

Spinoza knew that he was facing a life of loneliness, scorn and poverty. He was giving up a comfortable conformity in order to strive for something as intangible and seemingly unreachable as The Truth. He changed his name to Benedict and began to take care of his simple worldly needs by making and polishing lenses for the spectacles, microscopes and telescopes which were coming into popular use. He was never the healthiest man to begin with, and the glass dust endemic to his trade contributed to the consumption that would ultimately claim his life. But Spinoza could not be concerned about the weak vessel of his body. Rather, he was focused upon the thoughts that were swirling around in his mind.

Only one of Spinoza's works would be published in his lifetime; the ruling powers of Europe were as hostile to his ideas as had been the Jews of Amsterdam. For Spinoza, who would eventually be enshrined as the father of modern philosophy, was proposing that God and nature were indeed one. This concept was dangerously close to pantheism—the idea that creation was not depicted in the Bible, and Divine Providence was so much fantasy.

Except for a circle of friends, first in Rijnsburg and Voorburg, and then in The Hague (where he died), his philosophy was considered heresy and blasphemy. But Spinoza could not be diverted from his quest—and that was to find the true and lasting good, one that would so completely fill the mind that there would be no need for anything else. He quickly concluded and proved that power, sensual enjoyment and wealth (he had cut himself off from his family's benefience) were only transitory satisfactions that would never fulfill the deepest human desires. There was a higher good. Some of Spinoza's writings resonate with those of yearning mystics in conveying a search for unity with God. "I wonder if there is something that I could find and lay hold of, that might enable me to enjoy a perpetual and complete satisfaction."

Spinoza was dogged and incorruptible in his search. Once, when a coat was offered him, he refused it with the words, "Would I then become a different man? It is a bad thing when a sack is better than what it contains." He was a virtual recluse, alone with his ideas in a sparsely furnished room, taking the simplest of meals. As his fame spread, students wanted to study with him—and this would have provided a better income—but Spinoza refused. He would have had to teach a philosophy different from his own and, as his own was still forming, he knew it needed time to germinate, time alone and without distraction. He was offered a prestigious professorship in philosophy at the University of Heidelberg. This too he refused, so that he might continue to work unencumbered.

He saw his life's work clearly as a mission—not unlike that of clergy who tended souls or physicians who tended the sick. "A dying man foresees his certain death if no remedy is found, and uses all his strength to find some medicine, even a doubtful one; for upon it rests his only hope." He had to make the God of Scripture the God of life.

While Spinoza struggled to understand his God, so that he might worship him in confidence and security, he was the victim of continual disparagement. After one of his works appeared anonymously, it was soon linked to him and called a writing "Forged in hell by a renegade Jew and the devil. . . ."

He was frail and gaunt, but absolutely fearless:

> I think that I do not know within what limits that freedom of philosophizing ought to be confined in order to avoid the appearance of wishing to disturb the publicly established religion. For schisms arise not so much from an ardent love of religion as from men's various dispositions, or the love of contradiction, through which they are wont to distort and to condemn all things, even those that have been correctly stated.

And yet, there are wonderful stories of him as a person. Here was this towering intellect to whom the only proper pursuit of God was through informed reason, answering the question of his landlady: was her faith sufficient for her to be saved? "Your faith is good," he replied. "You do not need to seek for any other one in order to be saved, if only you lead a quiet and God-fearing life."

For the last 15 years of his life, Spinoza labored over the work for which he would be best known. And when it was completed, he knew that it could be published only after his death. The massive work was called *Ethics,* but it was far more than moral philosophy. Spinoza rested his conclusions on 295 propositions, ranging from an understanding of God, to a psychologically prescient theory of ideas to a stunning treatment of reason and the emotions. Spinoza's propositions ultimately became the sturdy columns upon which much of modern philosophy would be built. In the final portion of *Ethics,* Spinoza concludes that morality rests with each individual—never in the "goods" and "evils" of dogma—and that each person, only by understanding his or her own reason and emotions, can ultimately find happiness. And God.

With his *Ethics* Spinoza had come full circle, back to the point from which he had launched his quest. He had traveled the risky path of intellectual freedom, guided only by the best instincts he knew—instincts which would be proved and codified only in later life. He was at last able to name the good of which there was no better: the intellectual love of God which so filled the mind that it craved nothing more. In his lifetime, he was called an atheist; a hundred years after his death, he was termed "a man drunk with God."

He had liberated philosophy from theology once and for all; he had emancipated reason. Philosophy and

Spinoza

science could no longer be amended or dismissed because of the supposed moral power exercised by any religious authority. His work on the Bible opened up the field of higher criticism of holy writings. He did not discount the stories of Scripture, but saw them as allegories of deeper truths ingeniously fitted to the needs of the ancients. His stand for freedom of thought in political matters became the mighty force that would eventually end the church's role in state affairs.

For a century after his death, Spinoza's works went largely unnoticed. In order to preserve his independence, he had worked in almost total isolation. He had founded no school, prepared no followers. But in the 19th century his philosophical method began to receive the attention it deserved. A religious rebirth had begun and people looked for a God beyond strict dogma, a God linked with nature; a God attuned not to ritual alone, but to the deep groaning of the soul; a God working within the world.

This was the God Spinoza had helped to reveal.

Thus the road to true happiness which I have pointed out lies far removed from the great thoroughfare, and the ascent seems steep and difficult. And yet one should be capable of finding that path and following it. For verily, that which is so rare must be full of difficulties. If salvation were attained easily and without hardship, not so many would miss the path or decide to retrace their steps so soon. But surrounding the Sublime are ramparts and trenches that do not permit free passage to anyone without a great battle.

Companions Along the Way

Allison, Henry E., *Benedict de Spinoza,* Twayne, Boston, 1975.

Kayser, Rudolf, *Spinoza: Portrait of a Spiritual Hero,* Philosophical Library, New York, 1946.

Levin, Dan, *Spinoza: The Young Thinker Who Destroyed the Past,* Weybright & Tally, New York, 1970.

Pollock, Frederick, *Spinoza, His Life and Thought,* C. Kegan Paul, London, 1880.

Spinoza, Baruch (Benedict)—*The Chief Works of Spinoza,* 2 vols, trans by R.H.M. Elwes, Dover, New York, 1951.

Wienpahl, Paul, *The Radical Spinoza,* New York University Press, New York, 1979.

Harriet Tubman

She was a most unlikely heroine. Harriet Tubman was considered the lowest of the low—a dumb slave. Yet one thing never made sense to her: how, when it came to human beings, there could be owners and owned. With her daring escapes, she brought many slaves to freedom and helped break the chains of bondage.

CHILDHOOD was unkind to Harriet Tubman. Not only did her mistress keep a braided rawhide whip handy—and use it whenever Harriet might not dust the furniture correctly or inadvertently drop a dish—but Harriet was also the butt of jokes for other slave children. She seemed so dim-witted and slow. For no apparent reason at all, she would go into a dream-like trance and seemingly fall asleep. Her head drooped; her dazed, blood-shot eyes stared vacantly at the ground.

Companions Along the Way

She was a sturdy enough girl; one of ten children in her family, she was born about 1820. Unlike the other little girls, who were happy to work indoors, she hated household chores. She wanted at least the freedom of being outdoors and so would work in the forests with her father, who was hired out as a wood cutter. She put up with insults and abuse as her owner—already with more slaves than needed—hired her out to whomever would pay the pittance she could command.

But beneath this benign exterior was a woman with a determined and fertile mind. Harriet Tubman never forgot the day she tried to keep her master from beating another slave—and for interceding was struck in the head with a two pound grocer's weight, knocking her unconscious and nearly killing her. She never forgot the beatings she received at the hand of Miss Susan. She could hear the wails of children torn from their parents' arms and led off in shackles after they had been sold. She waited in a sullen silence.

Slavery was wrong; she knew that, most slaves in the American South knew that. But what could be done about it? Slaves could take out their hostility by stealing a cookie or plunging a finger into the fine china sugar bowl, by letting a baby cry or doing the work assigned just fast enough to avoid a whipping; but the sun set and rose and they were still slaves. There were wonderful stories going around—could they be true? Men like Nat Turner and his band who meted out death to the white man who kept them down. Slaves who had taken the famous Underground Railroad north to freedom. Blacks in the North who had good paying jobs, their own businesses, a real home; black children who went to school. But on Maryland's Eastern Shore, where Tubman lived, these seemed like fairy tales.

Not for Harriet Tubman. She had no use for the "loyal" or "faithful" slave and was never one herself. She saw no protection or benevolence in her overseers— as many slaves rationalized—only oppression and injustice. How could it be right that, for the slightest infractions (or merely to assert their power), masters could beat the slaves and the slaves had no recourse? What sense did it make that people could be bought and sold like livestock, the strongest and best-trained bringing the highest price?

The decisive moment came in 1849, when Tubman was 25 years old. Her master had died and his heirs were about to divide and sell her family out of state. If she died trying, she would die, but she was not going to be treated like chattel. She knew nothing of the North and had only heard of "Pennsylvania" and "New Jersey" but it was north she was heading. In one of her trances she saw horsemen coming and women and children screaming. And she saw ". . . a line, and on the other side of that line were green fields, and lovely flowers, and beautiful white ladies, who stretched out their arms to me over the line, but I couldn't reach them nohow. I always fell before I got to the line."

Harriet was married to a freed slave. Yet not only was her husband unwilling to leave, he threatened to expose her. Her three brothers started out with her, but soon turned back. Following the North Star by night, she crept through wood and swamp. On cloudy nights, she felt the moss that grew on the north side of trees. If there had been signs to see, they would have done her no good. Like most slaves she was illiterate. By day she slept—sometimes in a hideout that sympathizers offered to escaping slaves, sometimes with no more shelter than an overhanging tree or the safety of a cave.

Harriet Tubman had always been a woman of deep religious faith. Her God was not a wrathful judge who peered down on her, but a friend to whom she talked every day. He spoke to her in dreams and during those trances she suffered after the blow to her head. She was not given to prayers at regular times of the day, or on a special day of the week. When she felt a need, she simply trusted it to God to set the matter right. On that trip, He was her guide, she always maintained.

He would continue to be her guide in the years and trips ahead.

She finally arrived in Philadelphia and took jobs as a maid. She had her freedom and was able gradually to accumulate some money, but it wasn't enough. Slavery was still a reality for her family, her friends, for most black people in the South.

For a decade, Harriet Tubman performed one of the most extraordinary, continuing rescue missions in black history. She traveled back and forth no less than 19 times, bringing slaves to freedom on the Underground Railroad. This escape route was neither underground nor a railroad. Rather, it was an arduous, perilous journey overland, where any stranger could be the bounty hunter who turned you in, earning the thanks of the slave owner and a handsome reward.

Tubman was a cagey leader. She always left on a Saturday night, because wanted posters weren't printed on

Harriet Tubman

Sunday. Her days tracking in the woods at the Maryland plantation gave her an innate sense of direction—and potential danger. She was a backwoods nurse who knew the healing power of plants and herbs. She could set a bone or deliver a baby. When her fellow travelers said they couldn't walk another step, she urged them on. If they insisted, she pulled out the gun she carried and convinced them they had no choice but to go on.

She was so successful because, with her plain looks and drab clothes, she easily passed for an ordinary, faceless slave. If people considered her dim-witted, all the better. If her trances made them laugh and dismiss her as a sleepy good-for-nothing, she did nothing to counter their assessment of her. But on the march, she performed like a general leading her troops. She became known as the Moses of her people because, like that hero of the Old Testament, she guided her people from bondage to the promised land. She had women dress as men, men as women. They were stowed away in wagons; they carried falsified papers that showed they were free.

When she met John Brown, the two found both their religious beliefs and philosophies were alike. They were tired of the sincere but ineffective proclamations of the Abolitionists who offered little beyond their words. Together they planned the raid on Harper's Ferry; Tubman able to give Brown precise geographic information, Underground Railroad stops, as well as the names of freed slaves whom he could recruit. Only an illness prevented Tubman from being with Brown on that ill-fated day.

There is considerable speculation about Tubman's trances, her messages from God, the dreams in which she envisioned the safe route to take. Of course, they could have been exactly as Tubman reported them. But with our understanding of human psychology, as well as the information that has come down through the ages about mystics and seers, could it not also be the product of a deep meditation by a woman so sure of her God, so intent upon her mission? Harriet Tubman prayed for guidance. And she was sure it would come from her constant Companion.

She became a heroine to the Abolitionists in the North —Ralph Waldo Emerson and Frederick Douglass among them—and while she had no formal education, she was equally at home having a cup of tea in a Boston townhouse sitting room or speaking before a large audience in New York. She dressed in coarse but neat clothing. She loved to smile even though her upper front teeth were missing. There was a simplicity, a straight-forwardness about Harriet Tubman that was enormously appealing. To hear her tell of the narrow escapes she had experienced or of the continuing indignities suffered by slaves was—if one had any lingering doubts—to be converted to the anti-slavery movement. Her powerful speeches called not for an understanding of slavery, but its end. And she saw beyond, calling for the establishment of the rights of women, under law, regardless of their color.

But even in the North, Harriet Tubman couldn't completely rest—not even in Philadelphia, called the "Grand Central Station" of the Underground Railroad. Because of her work and the growing number of escaping slaves, the Fugitive Slave Law was reinforced in 1850; now escaped slaves could be captured and returned to the South. Tubman began taking her runaways all the way to Canada, where slavery was outlawed.

Tubman was so feared by slave owners that there was a $40,000 reward offered for her capture. Not only was she depriving the owners of what they considered their rightful property, she brought chaos to the entire institution of slavery. If a mere woman could, time after time, spirit away their slaves, no owner was safe. Abolitionists as well as slaves could take heart. She helped an estimated 300 slaves to freedom, but her impact was far wider than this. She achieved mythic proportions. She vowed to bring down this enemy of human decency, whatever the cost, whatever the tactic required.

With the outbreak of the Civil War, Harriet Tubman went immediately to the battle grounds. First she worked as a nurse, aiding the wounded on both sides. Tubman could talk to both sides—the slaves and to the soldiers —and secure the food and medicine that saved countless lives.

Seeing her unique abilities, the Union forces engaged her as a scout and a spy. As the war progressed, she began to sneak behind Confederate lines to report on troop movements. At this time, neither women nor blacks were permitted induction into the Union Army. She was a natural guerilla fighter, trained as she was during her many trips on the Underground Railroad. If needed, she could act like a loyal slave and denounce the North. If the situation called for it, she could (and did) take a band of black soldiers and destroy a supply depot.

For four years she served her country well, but with

the end of the Civil War, Harriet Tubman was quickly forgotten. Secretary of State William Seward petitioned Congress for a monthly pension of $20 for this war heroine, but eventually and begrudgingly eight dollars a month was allowed—a widow's pension, because her husband had died in the war.

Harriet Tubman was by now used to such indifference and racism. She tiredly smiled that toothless grin and carried on. She moved to Auburn, New York and, living close to poverty herself, opened her tiny house to poor and sick blacks, eventually opening a separate home for them. Although she had never had a day's schooling, she promoted the establishment of schools for the newly freed slaves in the South. Auburn became a shrine for the Abolitionists and to famous blacks—like Booker T. Washington, the outstanding black voice in America —who came to visit her. Eventually a book was written about her life and the proceeds were handed over to Tubman. For once, she had in hand over $1,000. But she was a person who saw no reason for saving money in a world where people were starving and had no place to live. She immediately used the money in her work and was poor once more herself.

When the book came out, Frederick Douglass wrote Tubman:

> You ask for what you do not need when you call upon me for a word of commendation. I need such words from you far more than you can need them from me. . . . The difference between us is very marked. Most that I have done and suffered in the

Harriet Tubman

service of our cause has been in public, and I have received much encouragement at every step of the way. You, on the other hand, have labored in a private way. I have wrought in the day—you in the night. I have had the applause of the crowd and the satisfaction that comes of being approved by the multitude, while the most that you have done has been witnessed by a few trembling, scared, and foot-sore bondmen and women, who you have led out of the house of bondage, and whose heartfelt 'God Bless You' has been your only reward.

Harriet Tubman struggled from day to day to meet the needs of the people who came to her. Eventually she became a vegetable peddler in the Auburn area, selling the produce from the gardens she maintained with those who could work. She died in 1913, in the home she had founded to care for sick and destitute blacks. A year later the people of Auburn unveiled a bronze tablet to her memory. Newspaper accounts noted that the audience at the ceremony was largely white. It was something unheard of at the time: whites honoring a black.

But Harriet Tubman stood for something beyond the color of a person's skin. She fought long and unflinchingly for human dignity and worth, qualities so universal and so fragile that their true defenders always transcend the artificial barriers, whatever they might be.

Bradford, Sarah H., *Harriet Tubman, the Moses of Her People,* Peter Smith, Gloucester, MA, 1981.

Companions Along the Way

Bradford, Sarah H., *Scenes in the Life of Harriet Tubman,* W.J. Moses, Printer, 1869 (reprinted, Books for Libraries Press, Freeport, New York, 1971).

Conrad, Earl, *Harriet Tubman,* Paul S. Eriksson, New York, 1943.

Heidish, Marcy, *A Woman Called Moses* (novel based on Tubman's life) Houghton-Mifflin, Boston, 1976.

II. Struggling to Find a Way

Jane Addams

George Herbert

Abraham Heschel

Aldous Huxley

Jane Addams

Privilege and poverty. A tumultuous era in American history. Heroine and villain. Jane Addams, that dour-faced woman who merits at least a few paragraphs in every grade school social history book, experienced it all. This companion, who most people know about— but few people know— merits a closer look.

IT WAS A popular tourist attraction for wealthy travelers during their stay in London: a visit to the Saturday night auction of spoiling food, the leftovers from the markets that week. The poor of London's East End, their hands waving, screamed out to the auctioneer so that their few pence might win them a crate of wilted cabbage, a pile of overripe tomatoes.

Jane Addams looked out over the teeming mass of slum-dwellers. While the other ladies and gentlemen quite enjoyed the spectacle, she could not. She had been on an extended tour of the continent and England and while traveling between her hotel and the fine restaurants and historic landmarks of Italy, France and Greece, she had also seen the ghastly underside of urban life. She had been raised in a wealthy family of upright Quakers in the rural midwest, and had gone on to college—a rarity for young women before the turn of the century. But now, in her early 20s, a seemingly perfect life was hollow, meaningless. She had everything to live with, but lacked a purpose to live for. The vacant faces of the poor kept flooding into this psychic vacuum. Their ragged clothing, their miserable hovels haunted her.

The year was 1883 and, as history would prove, it was a time in which the world—and especially America—would witness tremendous upheaval. Mass scale industrialization and a flood of immigrants from Europe would transform America, a country barely recovering from a civil war, into a giant among nations. And, in the process, family life would be forever altered. Women, traditionally in the home, would see their secure domain crumble. Merely to subsist they had to work outside the home in this new strange land, whose language they could not speak, whose customs made no sense. Their intact communities from the Old Country were but memories; they were forced to live in forbidding tenements or were jammed with their families into a ramshackle company house.

While the vast majority of American women were concerned about their very survival, Jane Addams was one of the few who had the leisure—and the liability —of time. Women of her background could do as they wanted, filling their lives with the gentle diversions and social obligations of the upper class. While a good number of this first wave of college-educated women somehow wanted more, they could not find a place to utilize their fertile minds, something to devote their energies to. They were a generation adrift, unwilling to merely be wives and mothers, yet prohibited from moving easily in the world dominated by men. No wonder ennui and depression were common complaints, that menstruation was an agony that women took to bed. The immigrant wife could not think of giving in to her body; for many an affluent woman, menstruation was a muted monthly cry of rage and frustration.

At Rockford Seminary, where Jane Addams was educated, there was enormous pressure for the young ladies not only to be "converted" Christians, but eventually to become missionaries. While she certainly had an affinity for the faith of her family, it was not *the* driving force in her life. One instructor provided an answer that made enormous sense to her: "I do not think we are put into the world to be religious, we have a certain work to do, and to do that is the main thing." But deciding what that work would be tortured Jane Addams.

She was subject to a spate of psychosomatic illnesses and undefined bouts of depression for some ten years after she graduated from college, but slowly what she had seen in slums of America and Europe began to coalesce with a deeper knowledge of her own temperament. It would be inaccurate to call that night in London or any other isolated incident that she experienced a singularly revelatory moment in the life of Jane Addams. Not many people, like Saul of Tarsus, are struck blind and talked to by God. It was more gradual for her; awareness came in simple forms. For instance, she found out, while recovering from an illness, that she could take care of children and not only not feel depleted but better for the effort. She enjoyed talking to old black women at a retirement home or working with poor children at a sewing school more than the diversion of a lecture or art exhibit. "Nervous people do not crave rest but activity of a certain kind," her friend Ellen Star said of the Jane Addams she had come to understand.

Jane Addams during her college years had righteously averred that the conquered South should be treated "with justice not mercy." She had condemned tramps: ". . . where they come from and whither they go is a conjecture, we only know they are trying to evade the principle set down from the foundations of the earth, that a just man give a full equivalent for everything he receives; by disregarding this principle they render themselves abject and mean and merit universal contempt."

But when she began to realize what a poor person really faced day to day, she could be righteous no longer.

Without an idea of exactly what they would do, Addams and Star moved into the dilapidated Hull mansion on Halsted Street in the middle of Chicago's overcrowded and predominantly poor West Side. Out of curiosity, neighborhood women came by to see what these two women, in dresses none of them could afford, were up to. Some brought their children, for whom this was an exciting diversion from the bleak street life they knew. It didn't take long for the two women to figure

Jane Addams

out that a kindergarten for these wide-eyed youngsters was a good place to start.

"The scheme," as Addams and Star called their yet unformed assault on poverty, grew as needs presented themselves. Cooking and sewing classes were started, a boy's club that not only included sports but the reading of classics, women's clubs where the needs of husband and family could be put aside, a boarding house for single working girls, courses in industrial trades. Bringing their own backgrounds and education to bear, the two women continually sensed other needs beyond the immediate. They started a Shakespeare club where weary wives and shopgirls could hear the immortal words, read and attend the plays. Other plays were routinely staged with the people of the neighborhood as the actors and actresses. Hull House, as the place was called, eventually had the first public baths in Chicago, a library, a dispensary which sold drugs at low cost and even a coalyard to provide inexpensive fuel.

The scope of Hull House's activities was impressive, but equally so was the involvement that Addams fostered in other wealthy and talented women. It was not uncommon for a rich woman to travel from Chicago's fashionable North Shore to run a Hull House program —and pay all the expenses. Addams accurately saw that while people might be "over cultured" and overeducated, they could still be living undernourished lives involved, as they were, only with themselves. Such were people "whose uselessness hangs about them heavily," she said. Experts in fields from children's creative play to American literature, to medicine and dentistry, willingly gave their time.

Companions Along the Way

Jane Addams—listening only to her own best instincts and to the cry of the humanity about her—had stumbled upon a concept that spread to the industrialized cities of America. Soon, settlement houses, based on Addams' work, were cropping up in poor areas across the country.

But there was more than social work going on as Addams' programs grew over the years. She was adamant about that. She observed, "It is curious how children catch the glow of the moral enthusiasm of their elders and absorb opinions by listening even though the issue touches them remotely." She knew that seeing only to bodily needs was never enough; Jane Addams was at work on people's souls. If a child was raised in a crowded, dirty tenement or sent to work in a noisy, dangerous factory, the results were all too predictable. On the other hand, she saw an irresistible and native desire within children to be good, if only the circumstances and the adults around them would allow it. She gave thousands of children that chance.

Although she was only nominally religious, and at times irreligious, Jane Addams had a profound impact on the way people lived their lives after being helped by her or working with her. Slum children went on to higher education and many into the helping professions. Idealistic co-workers came to her and, their idealism tested and firmly rooted, went on to important jobs in government and at colleges at a time when women were making their first significant inroads.

Beyond Hull House, Addams was a dominant national figure. She was instrumental in seeing child labor laws enacted; she almost single-handedly caused a revol-

Jane Addams

ution in criminal justice by urging that juvenile offenders be separated and treated differently than adults. Jane Addams came to symbolize the movement for social justice in America. Not only was she on the annual list of the ten Most Admired Women in the country, she often was at the top.

Jane Addams liked these accolades; she was hardly one to keep her light under the proverbial basket. But she was also able to confess mistakes she had made at Hull House. A deserted child had been taken to the nursery and despite expert medical attention, died. Her work of mercy over, Addams was ready to have the child buried by the county. When word of this got around the neighborhood, a collection was quickly taken up so that in death this child would at least have the dignity of a proper burial. "We were only forgiven by the most indulgent on the grounds that we were spinsters and could not know a mother's heart," she wrote.

Addams, while helping the people of her neighborhood, was not always tolerant of those she thought could do more for themselves. She often told a story on herself. An unemployed shipping clerk came to her during the depression of 1893 asking for help. She gave him some food and also told him that workers were being hired for work on a drainage canal. He said he couldn't work outdoors in winter, but Addams insisted he try. He worked two days, contracted pneumonia and died, leaving a wife and two young children. ". . . I cannot see them without a bitter consciousness that it was at their expense I learned that life cannot be administered by definite rules and regulations; that wisdom to deal with a man's difficulties comes only through some knowledge of his life and

69

habits as a whole; and that to treat an isolated episode is almost sure to invite blundering.'' In her mind the poor were not necessarily the willfully dependent, but rather those who in ''the unequal battle of modern industry'' had not triumphed.

Jane Addams was at the peak of her popularity in the years before World War I, and while her pacifist writings such as *Newer Ideals of Peace* were widely applauded by the like-minded, they were often ignored by most of the people who voted her an outstanding woman. But the war changed America's perception of their heroine.

In her speeches and writings, she often drew parallels between urban and military ills, saying that cities relied on ''penalties, coercion, compulsion, remnants of military codes to hold the community together.'' A strong advocate of woman's special role as peacemaker, she painted a grisly picture of men who bore arms. ''All kindness is illicit on the part of the military sentinel on duty.'' His object was the breakdown of ''morals on both sides, of the enforcer of ill-adapted law, as well as of those against whom it is so maladroitly directed.''

Battles raged in Europe, men died and were hailed as heroes, but Addams would not be drawn into such patriotism. In one speech, she told of the drugs and alcohol that were given to bayonet-wielding soldiers to bolster their courage before a charge. It was front-page news the next day and the subject of scathing editorials. She was called a ''silly, vain, impertinent old maid . . . now meddling with matters far beyond her capacity.'' Addams held her ground:

It is possible that the appeals for the organization

70

of the world along peaceful lines have been made too exclusively to man's sense of justice quite as the eighteenth century enthusiasm for humanity was prematurely founded on intellectual sentiment. Reason is only a part of the human endowment, emotion and deep-set radical impulses must be utilized as well, those primitive urgings to foster life and to protect the helpless, of which women were the earliest custodians . . . these universal desires must be given opportunities to expand and the most highly trained intellects must serve them rather than the technique of war and diplomacy.

Jane Addams seemed sadly out of step with her times, naive—and moreover a threat to national security. Once called a saint, she was now vilified as "the most dangerous woman in America." She had stood for what was best in America; now she represented the worst kind of citizen: disloyal in time of war. She was not only denounced as a communist, but "the reddest of the red." Her once-popular speeches were now found to be clarion calls to radicalism and pacifism. Because of her stature as a champion of the poor, she was all the more insidious, her critics said.

After the war, there was a significant change in working with the needy. Settlement houses like Hull House began to look terribly amateurish as the field of social work became professionalized and psychiatric treatment became more widespread. Again, Jane Addams looked out of step, advocating community involvement and social reform, and not what she considered a coldly rational approach to people. It was the Roaring 20s and

Companions Along the Way

America no longer honored the matronly Miss Addams but promoted a new kind of ideal woman—young and daring, with bobbed hair and saucy talk. No longer did scores of young people stream to Hull House to work. No longer was Jane Addams, a Victorian lady all her life, a role model.

When she was awarded the Nobel Prize for Peace in 1931, people were forced to take another, longer look at the life of Jane Addams. While some continued to criticize her, most assessments of her many decades of settlement house work, her drive for world peace, and her efforts toward the enactment of social legislation concluded that this was a woman who had stood the test of time; she was praised for her "unyielding fight for her ideals." And when she died in 1935, Walter Lippman wrote: "She had compassion without condescension. She had pity without retreat into vulgarity. She had infinite sympathy for common things without forgetfulness of those that are uncommon."

When Jane Addams was born, Abraham Lincoln was running for president; at her death, the New Deal was in full swing. During those years, she addressed virtually all of the crucial issues of the day: poverty, immigration, labor organizing, housing reform, child labor legislation, feminism. She helped transform America's conscience from that of a frontier, laissez-faire mentality to one where caring for the less fortunate became embodied in law.

Her range is indeed daunting. But, as with all the Companions, it's important not just to look at the accomplishments, for this is not the measure of a person's life. (Albert Schweitzer left a 70-building medical com-

72

Jane Addams

pound; Charles de Foucauld, a hut and few tatters of clothing.) And it is important to cast a critical eye on what is written about the person—and *by* them.

So often an autobiography of a famous person appears seamless, as if the events in their life were so loaded with meaning at the time, their progress so steady, their goals so apparent. We read such books and reflect: my life is not so neat; I'm doing the best I can, but I hardly see any effect. Progress? Goals?

It's more important to look at what compelled and drove a woman like Jane Addams. She made a conscious decision to help the people of Chicago's West Side, but her actions were not part of some grand plan. Rather, Jane Addams matched her inner resources to the immediate needs she saw about her. She applied the basic Christian impulses she had learned as a child and in school in a direct and daily way. She certainly possessed a spirituality, but it was a practical spirituality.

And regardless of praise or condemnation, she just kept on going.

Addams, Jane, *Twenty Years at Hull House,* Macmillan, New York, 1910.

_____, *Newer Ideals of Peace,* Macmillan, New York, 1907.

Davis, Allen F., *American Heroine: The Life and Legend of Jane Addams,* Oxford, New York, 1973.

Levine, Daniel, *Jane Addams and the Liberal Tradition,* State Historical Society of Wisconsin, Madison, 1971.

George Herbert

George Herbert knew well the lure of worldly ambition and yet he found his true fulfillment far from the great halls of Cambridge where his voice was resoundingly heard or the chambers of Parliament where he once sat. He has something to say about the inner yearning to do something worthwhile that so many people feel throughout their lives—and die never having done it.

O N THE third of March, 1633, in the tiny English village of Bemerton in Wiltshire, the parson's casket was borne across the narrow cobblestone road that separated the rectory—where he had died two days before—from the church, St. Andrew's, where he had served. Although beloved by the simple rural folk of Bemerton for the short time he had been with them, his had otherwise not been a particularly successful life. In fact, though the parishioners would have angrily stood nose to nose with anyone who might have uttered the thought, for a man as high born and well educated as he, it might even have been considered a dismal failure.

He had been given a seat in Parliament, but lasted only one session. He had received an excellent appointment as an orator at Cambridge, but fouled it up badly, criticizing the very man upon whom he was paid to heap praise. A few of his poems had been published—but only in Latin and Greek. He was, by all accounts, an unknown. Once deemed a promising young man at the Royal Court in London, he had died in a village so pathetically small it is often left off maps.

Pastor George Herbert had come to Bemerton less than three years before and from the day he arrived, the people had wondered how long the thin, tall, rather sickly-appearing parson would stay, how long he could withstand the banality and lowliness of their way of life. Their church was in a sad state of disrepair, the altar vestments in tatters. Their souls were equally rundown. Puritan fanaticism, virulent in those days, had castigated them for their wretched sinfulness. They had believed too much of it. The townspeople were embarrassed; they could barely meet Mr. Herbert's eyes that first day he walked about the village and reached out to shake their hands.

But something magical happened during those years. Pastor Herbert repaired their church and healed their souls. He inspired and warmed them with his at once stirring and yet straightforward sermons, his friendly visits, his modest but exemplary demeanor. He was always so kind, understanding, charitable; how was it that from the beginning, he knew so well the innermost secrets and yearnings of their souls? If he had a harsh word, it was for the selfish or the lazy—and never for them. He spoke of God's love in a fresh and real way; and they, in turn, felt loved when they were in his presence.

At times they could see him through the study window writing at his desk, his usually serene face strained, contorted almost as if he were in pain. As few of them could read or write, they made little of it. Studying all those tiny letters or holding a quill in such a strange position for hours at a time—that was probably why he looked that way.

The burial service that March morning in Bemerton was held with all due reverence and Pastor Herbert's body was laid to rest beneath the altar. A gravestone was put in place. At his request, as he had felt his life so uneventful and unavailing, there was no inscription on it.

And so might have ended the story of George Herbert, only to be remembered by those who knew him, perhaps recalled by their children and then forgotten as are most of the dead. But, just before he died, George Herbert dictated a will and passed along a small sheaf of his writings, instructing that they be shown to his good friend, Nicolas Ferrar. ". . . Desire him to read it; and then, if he can think it may turn to the advantage of any dejected poor soul, let it be made public: if not, let him burn it; for I and it are the least of God's mercies."

To our benefit, Ferrar persisted in having this unknown Anglican priest published. And today, George Herbert's "The Temple" stands as some of the most powerful and beautiful poetry ever written about a man's struggle to find and know his God, while his prose work, *The Country Parson* serves as the standard against which anyone entrusted with the care of souls might measure him or herself.

George Herbert, stumbling along in life, plagued by poor health and indecisiveness, unwittingly became the shining light of that most difficult period in Europe, the post-Reformation, and one of the greatest religious poets the world has known. Aldous Huxley praised him as the poet of "inner weather;" T.S. Eliot, very much a man of his time, looked back 300 years to Herbert to find a way of thinking and living out his newly found religious faith in our frenetic 20th century.

Eliot's selection of Herbert as his proper inspiration was certainly shrewd. For Herbert's time was no less complicated than Eliot's—or our own. It was an era of rapid expansion of knowledge—an information explosion—as well as religious unheaval. The fires of theological revolution that Luther and Calvin and the great reformers had kindled were now cooled, and the men and women of 17th century Europe were aswirl in a roiling sea of religious anarchy. The medieval, monolithic Catholic Church was dead, and self-appointed saviors roamed the countryside preaching everything from the death of organized religion to a vengeful God so displeased with the human experiment that He was ready to wipe it out. People were confused; doctrine and age-old rituals were suspect. Stained glass windows were shattered and Eucharist was banned in many churches to stamp out idolatrous superstition. The Church of England, after abruptly severing its ties with Rome, and struggling to find its own unique voice in this tumult, was plagued with infighting and indecision.

It's amazing to look back to that obscure village of Bemerton and realize that one man, living there for two and a half years, writing two books that were not published in his lifetime, could so profoundly embrace the best of basic Christian practice and beliefs—the rich soil in which so many had grown in faith—and incorporate so much of the new, emerging culture that allowed man and woman to question their God. In a way, Herbert was ideal for the task. Here was a man who knew about the windstorms of the soul—so many had raged in his own. And here was a man who equally realized (although he tried over and over to run from it) that there was no life worth living unless it grappled with the God of the universe.

It's even more amazing, realizing that George Herbert had no idea what he was doing. He was simply following his heart, listening to that gentle, inner voice and doing the simple things it urged.

George Herbert was born into this confusing period of history—there he had no choice—but he could have avoided the chaos that ensued in his life had he just followed in the footsteps of the men of his bloodline: knights, distinguished statesmen, great military leaders. A bright boy, as quick with his wit as he was in his school work, he appeared on his way to a successful career during his college days at Trinity College, Cambridge. He was named public orator at Cambridge. It was a pres-was named public orator at cambridge. It was a prestigious appointment, granting him such privileges as

George Herbert

walking alone in academic processions so that he might be seen and lauded, and the power to confer degrees on noblemen and their sons—whether or not they had bothered to attend a single class. His function as public orator was to write and deliver speeches, copiously thanking Cambridge benefactors and grandly extolling the virtues of the royal family. In a word, he was to be a 17th century public relations man for Cambridge, his calling to make artful flattery a high art. The rewards were generous for saying the right things about the right people; the two orators before him had gone on to high government posts.

The young George Herbert grandly filled the position. He dressed in expensive, finely tailored clothes, and casting aside the ancients, often quoted in his speeches the finest scientist of the day, Sir Francis Bacon, instead of Cicero, a safer and more usual choice. It was bold modernity at its best. Everyone thought George Herbert would certainly go a long way with such a combination of brilliance and flamboyance.

The public George Herbert was a smashing success. Only his closest friends knew that there was another man within those grand clothes, another voice besides the cultured, stentorian intonations for which he was so famous. From an early age George had felt an urge to serve God, but as his life went along, he convinced himself that he couldn't find the most suitable way, one that would utilize the many talents he knew he possessed. At the age of 17 he made some noises about continuing his studies and being ordained a priest of the Church of England, but he never followed through. A few years later, as a compromise, he grandly vowed to devote his poetical powers to God. At 24, he again announced himself ready for the priesthood. But it was so much talk.

As masterful as he was with words, constructing whatever rhetorical concoctions the moment called for, this rising young star of the English court was equally talented in manipulating his own emotions. At the time, faithful service to the crown was, in the best circles in London, considered as worthy a path to sanctity as the religious life—and Herbert smugly convinced himself that his was indeed a worthy, high calling. After all, he was a good, observant, church-going Anglican; he wasn't engaged in any illicit or illegal activities.

Herbert knew he was paying no more than lip service, going through the formalities of his faith and little more. But at each turn, when The Call to truly serve pounded at his ears, he let the world's siren song seduce him once more. He liked power, prestige and good living too much.

In 1624, following family tradition, he decided to take his place in Parliament. It was the perfect time to further his career with some legislative exposure. To the casual observer, the career of George Herbert was moving along swimmingly. It would seem he could sit for a few years in Parliament and, after that, do just fine in court with his elegant manners and demeanor, his way with words.

But, to the shock of his family and friends, George Herbert was to last no more than one session. In those corridors of power and influence, where men promoted both themselves and their favorite causes with apostolic zeal, where high-minded speeches forged shabby, self-serving political deals, Herbert found himself repelled.

George Herbert

He might have once more smiled, bowed and continued his membership in the club, but this time he found he couldn't.

Called upon to deliver a routine, congratulatory oration to Prince Charles, bent on war with Spain after a futile attempt to marry a Spanish princess, Herbert could maintain his public face no longer. He had to say what he felt, not what royalty wanted to hear. He soundly, albeit eloquently, lectured the bellicose prince about peace. Charles was not amused.

Obviously something was at work in the life of a man then 31 years old. He had burned some strategic bridges behind him. Then, the newly unpredictable Herbert took a step that completely astounded his contemporaries. He asked to be ordained a deacon of the Church of England. One of the provisions of the diaconate was that he could no longer hold any civil appointment. The career that once looked so promising was finished. Overnight, he lost both face and his circle of friends at court.

His life in shambles, facing an uncertain future, George Herbert sensed he had to stand in place and take seriously the words he had so often mouthed, but never fully lived: he would wait upon God to direct him. And while he waited, as much to clear his muddled mind as anything else, he wrote of his struggle to find God. He had no idea these poems would ever be published. At the time, his words were simply the outward, painful expressions—as best he could formulate them at the time—of the inarticulate sounds deep within his heart. These poems would eventually form the nucleus of what became the epic, "The Temple."

Herbert was 37 years old when he was finally given the

bedraggled church at Bemerton. It was in horrible condition, the parsonage barely habitable. But Herbert saw St. Andrew's as a metaphor for the Church itself: the man-made structure might be weak, but the God-given foundation was strong and right. It had to be rebuilt; the people, reconstituted. He knew, if he resorted to the dramatic oratorical flourishes of which he was so capable, he could convince the parishioners of virtually anything overnight, have them do his bidding, whatever that might be. But he was certain that his salvation and theirs depended not on a quick fix or pretty words. He knew that the vain George Herbert had to die and that a simple country parson, humble before God, had to take his place.

Herbert first saw to it that the church was fit for worship and the parsonage habitable for him and his new bride. Then, slowly and methodically, he began to instruct his congregation in the basic tenets of their faith. More importantly, he lived it out before their eyes. The poor were given clothes and food, not only by Herbert directly, but by their more fortunate neighbors, who followed the pastor's example. On his afternoon rounds, Herbert made it a point to visit every last member of his congregation, either at home or in their work place. And, each morning at 10 and afternoon at 4, Pastor and Mrs. Herbert unfailingly appeared in church for prayer. In the early days at Bemerton, they were often the only ones. But soon, at the sound of the church bell, farmers left their horses standing in the field and women left their rising dough on the breadboard so that they might join in community prayer.

George Herbert

It was not long before there was a new bounce in their step, a sparkle in their eyes. The church calendar came alive for them, the feasts were celebrations once more. Their lives had meaning and dignity. The Puritans be damned! Their God was not a hateful bookkeeper. They were loved by a merciful, compassionate, forgiving God, who showed His ways through the beauty of the world around them, the power of the church and community they had rebuilt—and through this man from London, who cared so desperately about each of them.

During a time of turmoil in Christendom, when intrachurch fighting had shattered many a congregation, George Herbert saw beyond the conflicts of his century and haled his parishioners back to the ways of Christ and the early Church.

He never glossed over the difficulties of life, never allowed his parishioners to escape from the fragility and brokenness of man's very existence on this earth. But he held up to them a strength equal to any assault or heartache—the Christian heritage, a Church united, a Savior whose concern for them knew no bounds and never flagged. And he brought those immortal truths home, not in the language of the educated, but in the currency of faith and everyday life.

As he wrote in "The Parson Catechising":

Doubtless the Holy Scripture intends this much, when it condescends to the naming of a plough, a hatchet, a bushel, leaven, boys piping and dancing; showing that things of ordinary use are not only to serve in the way of drudgery, but to be washed and cleansed, and serve for lights even of heavenly truths.

83

Companions Along the Way

Herbert knew he was as broken and fragile as any of the people who sat in the pews of St. Andrew's. And, so as continually to examine what he was doing—as he strove to bring about God's kingdom on earth and better understand himself and his motives—Herbert took out his sheaf of poems at Bemerton. He wrote new prose and poetry and rewrote old poems, expressing now with practical experience at his elbow what he had been trying to say over the years. Sometimes words came and often they didn't. He might ask a question in the first line of a verse and leave the answer blank, because he didn't know what to say. He suffered through the daily trials of life, prayed and—that most difficult of human tasks—waited still more. Scholars who study him today may be frustrated in a line-by-line analysis of his poetry; often he contradicts himself. But it is obvious Herbert was working with more than poetic vision. He begged for—and received—grace. He did the best he could, and put the rest in the hands of God to complete.

In a particularly moving stanza in "A True Hymn," God comes into that rectory study and participates with Herbert in composition:

> Whereas if th'heart be moved,
> Although the verse be somewhat scant,
> God doth supply the want.
> As when th'heart says (sighing to be approved)
> *O could I love!* and stops: God writeth, *Love.*

In person a most discreet and kindly man, Herbert stripped his soul bare upon the pages he wrote. He knew that for everyone life was a struggle and he wanted to be honest about his own. There is more than a hint of the Old Testament prophet in Herbert: his mood swings, utter confusion, open rebellion, periods of spiritual deadness, the frequent temptations to doubt. This famous, lyrical selection from "Affliction" might serve as a short biographical sketch of the man:

> At first thou gav'st me milk and sweetness;
> I had my wish and way:
> My days were straw'd with flow'rs and happiness;
> There was no month but May.
> But with the years sorrow did twist and grow,
> And made a party unawares for woe.

> My flesh began unto my soul in pain
> Sicknesses cleave my bones;
> Consuming agues dwell in ev'ry vein,
> And tune my breath to groans.
> Sorrow was all my soul; I scarce believed,
> Till grief did tell me roundly, that I lived.

A man who knew how good he wanted to be, but how often he failed, Herbert made clear from the beginning of *The Country Parson* that he was writing not autobiography, but a set of guidelines:

> . . . That I might have a mark to aim at: which also
> I will set as high as I can, since he shoots higher
> that threatens the Moon, than he that aims at a
> Tree.

Surely this book is the good fruit of his labors at Bemerton. Revered and referred to over the decades, *The Country Parson* has taken its place among the greatest of spiritual guides ever written. Herbert displays reverence for ceremony and doctrine, which are cherished by the most high church Catholics among his readers. Meanwhile, he calls upon each man and woman to look deeply in their souls, question themselves, talk to their God, use their reason as well as their faith —which has endeared him to the most liberal Protestant.

It is a practical guide, advising the parson, for instance, if he finds his members "religiously employed," he ". . . both commends them much. . . . (and) he furnisheth them with good books." And if they are working? ". . . he commendeth them also: for it is a good and just thing for everyone to do their own business." With Pastor Herbert, indeed, you were cherished and respected. Regardless.

When Izaak Walton wrote his biography shortly after Herbert's death, he highlighted his turn from the world and toward Bemerton, making it a dramatic apocalypse. Others, looking more critically at Herbert's life, have said it was simply a case of failed ambition that brought about his religious vocation. But as more and more study of Herbert is undertaken, it becomes clear that here was a man who all along knew deeply he had to find God in this life, but who had enormous difficulty seeing the path he should take.

He spent years in the secular world so that the few at Bemerton could be lived. In that fraction of his lifetime he found his true calling. And those scant years, serving the daily needs of a tiny rural congregation—as a failure to all those who knew him as the dapper, eloquent

George Herbert

orator—gave him a lasting authority that towers over whatever he might have accomplished in the larger arena of public life.

Benet, Diana, *Secretary of Praise: The Poetic Vocation of George Herbert,* Columbia, University of Missouri Press, 1984.

Charles, Amy Marie, *A Life of George Herbert,* Ithaca, NY, Cornell University Press, 1977.

Herbert, George, *The Works of George Herbert,* ed., F.E. Hutchinson, Oxford, Clarendon Press, 1941.

Hyde, A.G., *George Herbert and His Times,* London, Methuen, 1906.

Wall, John N., ed., *Priest to the Temple: The Country Parson and The Temple,* (Classics of Western Spirituality Series), Paulist Press, Mahwah, N.J., 1981.

Abraham Heschel

Too often people find the religion of their youth constricting. A foolish excess they relegate to younger and naive years. It seems to have no place or relevance in their later lives. Abraham Heschel found that he could take his strict religious upbringing not only into the world, but that he could share it with others and reach across the boundaries that separate people of various religious beliefs.

AS A BOY, when he would see one of his good friends on the streets of Jewish Warsaw, Abraham Heschel would burst out in laughter, unable to contain his happiness. Although he was considered a biblical scholar at the age of 10, young Abraham hardly seemed the scholarly type; his delight with the simplest daily occurrences was boundless. He loved the study of the Torah, the sight of a sunrise, the hours spent in temple worship; he loved the sight of a familiar face.

He was the son of an Hasidic rabbi, a descendant of the legendary Baal Shem Tov, the founder of the Hasidic movement, and his early life was rich in the culture, worship and observances of this strict but spirited branch of Judaism. His first book of poems he boldly entitled *Man, the Ineffable Name of God*. There was little doubt that Abraham was destined to continue in the long line of rabbis in his family.

But when he was ready to go on to higher education, he shocked the Jewish community with his decision to go first to Vilna and then to the University of Berlin. Heschel wanted to study and experience the world outside his closed environment. He wanted to drink of Western civilization, science, the arts. He was in love with his tradition, but at that point in his life, it seemed to impose boundaries on his development that he could not abide.

And, like many a college student before and after him, the years at the university were ones of unsettling internal struggle.

> I looked for a system of thought, for the depth of the spirit, for the meaning of existence. Yet in spite of the intellectual power and honesty which I was privileged to witness, I became increasingly aware of the gulf that separated my views from those held at

the university. . . . To them, religion was a feeling . . .
They spoke of God from the point of view of man
. . . They granted Him the status of being a logical
possibility . . . in Berlin I went through moments of
profound bitterness. I felt very much alone with my
own problems and anxieties. I walked alone in the
evenings through the magnificent streets of Berlin. I
admired the solidity of its architecture, the overwhelming drive and power of a dynamic civilization.
There were concerts, theatres, and lectures by famous scholars about the latest theories and inven-
tions . . .

Suddenly I noticed the sun had gone down, evening had arrived . . . I had forgotten God, I had
forgotten Sinai—I had forgotten that sunset is my
business—that my task is 'restore the world to the
Kingship of the Lord.' So I began to utter the words
of evening prayer.

'Blessed Art Thou, Lord Our God
King of the Universe
Who By His Word Brings on the Evenings . . .'

On that evening in the streets of Berlin, I was not
in a mood to pray. My heart was heavy, my soul was
sad. It was difficult for the lofty words of prayer to
break through the dark clouds of my inner life. But
how would I dare not to pray? How would I dare to
miss an evening prayer?

Heschel was not ready to return to the life in Warsaw,
but he was equally dissatisfied with himself as merely a
secular Jew. Yet as the years unfolded, he found that he
could incorporate his Hasidic side with that of a scholar,

Abraham Heschel

teacher and writer in the world. Many who have left Hasidism turn their back on it—cut their locks and their beard—and adapt to the ways of the world. Heschel was an anomaly in that he kept Hasidism in his heart, yet lived outside its community. Warsaw was the seed and the fertile soil; the world outside Warsaw would continue to stimulate Heschel and he would enrich it in return.

He was first Martin Buber's successor in Frankfurt, but with the ominous advance of Nazism he fled to London, where he established the Institute for Jewish Learning. He then came to America, where he taught in both Reformed and Orthodox Jewish seminaries. His vision was by now clear: to teach and to write, to combine the love of Judaism with love for the world and to proclaim the uniqueness of its traditions and thought.

After the war, while becoming well known within Jewish religious circles, Heschel was virtually unknown to other faiths. In 1951, with the publication of *God In Search of Man,* that changed. He proposed a radical idea—which crossed the boundaries of all faiths and which was unique in American theology—that "The Bible is primarily not man's vision of God but God's vision of man."

In *God In Search of Man,* Heschel writes:

> God's search for man, not man's quest for God was conceived to have been the main event in Israel's history . . . Israel's religion originated in the initiative of God rather than in the efforts of man . . . Man would not have known Him if He had not approached man. God's relation to man precedes man's relation to Him.

Companions Along the Way

Heschel's understanding came during a time when the prevailing view accented man's need for God. Heschel turned that around, going back to the rich but little known experience of Jewish mystics, who, through their fasting and ascetic lives in such places as Qumran, were

> . . . inspired by a bold and dangerously paradoxical idea that not only is God necessary to man but that man is necessary . . . to the unfolding of His plans in the world.

Such a God could not be a God belonging exclusively to Jew or Christian or Moslem, Heschel posited, but *the one God* who could not work in the world without his helpmates, man and woman. And such a God could not be calling on any one faith to preserve itself at all costs and to the detriment of other believers. Religion and faith took on new meaning at Heschel's hand:

> The cardinal problem is not the survival of religion, but the survival of man. What is required is a continuous effort to overcome hardness of heart, callousness, and above all to inspire the world with the biblical image of man, not to forget that man without God is a torso, to prevent the dehumanization of man. For the opposite of human is not the animal. The opposite of the human is the demonic.

While he remained a practicing Jew and was certainly not advocating some sort of watered down, creedless faith, Heschel constantly sounded the alarm against what he called "religious behaviorism." Religious deeds and pious practices could not be performed in a vacuum, hermetically sealed against the world. "The external action is the essential mode of worship," he proclaimed.

He saw his own Judaism as a religion of love, but a religion that also required its followers to take on a yoke. Judaism's God was a loving God, but also a demanding one. And, He was not a God to be reached by some sort of intellectual path:

> A Jew is asked to take a leap of action rather than a leap of thought. He is asked to surpass his needs, to do more than he understands in order to understand more than he does. . . . Through the ecstasy of deeds he learns to be certain of the hereness of God. Right living is a way to right thinking.

What was appealing about Heschel's approach was that while it embraced the exhilaration of his Hasidic background, and took for granted a loving God, it equally presupposed a life of sustained tension for the believer. Rhapsody did not mean comfort; this God of the ages who wanted a relationship with every man and woman had to be confronted and wrestled with every day. While people throughout the ages have tried to make religion into an island refuge, Heschel was for expanding, rather than confining. He was the first Jewish scholar appointed to the faculty at Union Theological Seminary and as the word "ecumenism" came into the vocabulary, Heschel promoted it with his usual common sense:

> Should we refuse to be on speaking terms with one another and hope for each other's failure? Or

should we pray for each other's health, and help one another in preserving one's respective legacy, in preserving a common legacy?

He was surely the most respected Jewish voice among Protestants and Catholics who were finally opening up to the richness of Judaism, a religion they had misunderstood and shunned for centuries. Heschel was popularly called the "Apostle to the Gentiles." His words knew no boundaries of sect and religious educators especially sought him as a speaker. In his best known speech to a group of Catholic educators, "Idols in the Temple," he said:

> What our young people need is not religious tranquilizers, religion as a diversion, religion as entertainment, but spiritual audacity, intellectual guts, power of defiance . . . In our classrooms we shy away from fundamental issues. How should one deal with evil? What is our relation to the enemy? What shall one do about envy? What is the meaning of honesty? . . . To teach means to impart information as well as to let the pupil share one's appreciation. The secret of religious education is learning, passion and conviction.

Heschel traveled and spoke widely in order to tell of the God in search of man and man's search for God. His was not a religion that was to be proclaimed to only the like-minded. His impact on a group of Bell Telephone middle managers, gathered for a seminar in the mid-1960s, is reflected in the words of one of the people there:

Abraham Heschel

The Bell System group was made up of middle-aged, gentile business executives, whose normal concerns were those of the corporation, and yet each member of the group was . . . struck by the aura of reverence, wisdom and concern for mankind which seemed to emanate from Rabbi Heschel. . . . I felt that his thoughts were communicated to me through a medium far beyond his words. If, when he had finished, he had risen and beckoned me to follow, I would have done so without question. Even after 15 years, I am convinced that, on that day, I sat with a Biblical prophet.

His presence was so powerful because here was a man who exuded belief in the presence of a *living* God, not some character safely restricted to the pages of pious books. Great deeds were possible because man never acted alone; this God who was constantly in search of him was always there. Heschel was a modern rabbi who made his ancient tradition real and many called him a "zaddik," the saint of his generation sent into the midst of ordinary mankind to reawaken people to a relationship with God they sorely needed. He spoke of prayer as

. . . spiritual ecstasy. . . . A keen single force draws our yearning for the utmost out of the seclusion of the soul. We try to see our visions in His light, to feel our life as His affair. We begin by letting the thought of Him engage our minds, by realizing His name and entering into a reverie which leads through beauty and stillness, from feeling to thought, and from understanding to devotion.

Companions Along the Way

Heschel's thoughts were so accessible to people, so reasonable and yet so profound, transmitting a visceral feeling, that, once experienced, made perfect sense. Wonder and awe were mainstays; the boy from the Warsaw ghetto had not lost his youthful appreciation:

> Mankind will not die for lack of information. It will perish for lack of appreciation. . . . The great marvel of being alive is the ability to discover the mystery and wonder of everything . . . Unless we learn how to revere, we will not know how to exist as human beings. . . .
>
> . . . Awe precedes faith; it is at the root of faith. We must grow in awe in order to reach faith . . . Awe rather than faith is the cardinal attitude of the religious Jew. . . .
>
> . . . This is the tragedy of every man: 'to dim the world by indifference.' Life is routine, and routine is resistance to the wonder . . . 'But a small hand held against the eye hides it all,' said the Baal Shem. 'Just as a small coin held over the face can block out the sight of a mountain, so can the vanities of living block out the sight of the infinite light.'

Heschel was not merely mouthing words when he said the person of faith had to bring beliefs into the world. As he could not abide intolerance and superiority of one group over another, he was an early and ardent advocate of the civil rights movement. At Selma, he was linked arm in arm with Martin Luther King on that famous march.

He was a powerful presence as an observer at the Second Vatican Council, assuring that the Church would acknowledge and proclaim in the council documents "the permanent preciousness of the Jewish people." When Pope Paul VI later told an audience that "Even before we have moved in search of God, God has come in search of us," he was echoing the essence of Heschel's thought.

As he grew to be an old man, he took on the cause of the elderly, another of the many disregarded groups he embraced in his lifetime:

> Being old is not necessarily the same as being stale . . . Old men need a vision, not only recreation. Old men need a dream, not only a memory. It takes three things to attain a sense of significant being:
> God
> A soul
> A moment
> And the three are always there.

Even in the last days of his life, though frail and in poor health, Heschel continued to speak out on social issues: civil rights, Vietnam, the plight of Soviet Jews, poverty. A few days before he died, and against his doctor's orders, he was standing outside a prison when a friend who was an anti-war activist was released. To the end, he was a prayerful, religious man who took those prayers and that faith into the world. Recovering from a near fatal heart attack, he summarized the role of God in his life: "I did not ask for success; I asked for wonder. And You gave it to me."

Shortly before his death in 1972, in an NBC interview,

he directed a message to young people confused and in turmoil because of the legacy of the Vietnam War and the social injustices about them:

> Remember that there is a meaning beyond absurdity . . . that every little deed counts, that every word has power, and that we can all do our share to redeem the world. . . . And above all, remember that the meaning of life is to build a life as if it were a work of art.

Heschel, Abraham Joshua, *God in Search of Man: A Philosophy of Judaism,* Farrar, Straus and Cudahy, New York, 1951.

_____, *Man's Quest for God: Studies in Prayer and Symbolism,* Scribner's, New York, 1954.

_____, *The Prophets,* Harper & Row, New York, 1962.

_____, *Who Is Man?,* Stanford University Press, Stanford, 1968.

Kasimow, Harold, *Divine-Human Encounter: A Study of Abraham Joshua Heschel,* University Press of America, Washington, 1979.

McBride, Alfred, *Heschel: Religious Educator,* Dimension Books, Denville, NJ, 1973.

Merkle, John C., ed., *Abraham Joshua Heschel: Exploring His Life and Thought,* Macmillan, New York, 1985.

Aldous
Huxley

So many of us feel so foolish, so scattered, so misdirected as we try to make ourselves better people, this world a better place. Aldous Huxley was all over the ballpark, too. But whether he was applauded or scorned for his current thinking, he went on doggedly, and, near the end of his life . . . well . . . let's join him in a speech given in the early 1960s.

"I T IS A little embarrassing that . . ."
The speaker peered out over the crowd through thick glasses, then down at his notes, scrawled in huge letters. One eye was slightly askew and blind; the other still transmitted images but not all that well. His voice was raspy from the cancer eating away at his tongue and spreading through his throat. Gangly, reed-thin and pale, he looked as though he might not be able to go on. ". . . .

after forty-five years of research and study, the best advice I can give to people. . . ."

Members of the overflow audience moved forward in their seats, straining to hear, anticipating what might come next from a man popularly considered one of the great minds of the 20th century. It was no secret this might be one of Aldous Huxley's last speeches and perhaps, just perhaps, the man who had spent much of his life in a dogged pursuit of authenticity, truth and spiritual transcendence might bring together the distillation of that journey. The 1960s were upon America, change was in the wind; people wanted a new direction. He looked up. The room was quiet as Huxley's lips began to move. The audience awaited their marching orders.

". . . the best advice I can give is, is to be a little kinder to each other."

Idolized as an inspired critic, then revered as a sage, dismissed as a foolish mystic, regarded as a man out of date with nothing new to say, there he stood, a weary traveler sure of only one thing: kindness. He knew how rough was the road to self-understanding and he wanted those companions in the audience trudging on their individual journeys to help each other along. Few have struggled so openly and covered such diverse intellectual, literary and spiritual terrain to make some sense out of this life, to find a way for the people of this planet to live in harmony. Huxley was more a reflector than a beacon of his time, a seismograph, not the earthquake. He will never be ranked with the great writers of the time, as for instance, Virginia Woolf. But while Woolf chronicled the torment of the age, Huxley went one difficult step further. He tried to show that healing would only come

Aldous Huxley

through application of that simplest of balms: genuine human concern.

Equally fascinated and perplexed by life's mysteries, he was hardly consistent; his views and the direction of his quest changed dramatically throughout his life. This witty satirist had also known deep despair; he tried hypnotism and psychedelic drugs; he had studied deeply the wisdom at the core of Christianity and the great religions of the East. And yet, there he stood, unresolved, facing death, still on the search—and humbly admitting how little he really knew.

And because of his unrelenting and what might be called by some an eventually fruitless search, Aldous Huxley holds a special place among the Companions. Battered but unbowed, he stands as the Patron Saint of the Perpetual Seeker.

He was a man nourished by two mighty streams. Through Matthew Arnold on his mother's side he was endowed with a great literary talent and from his grandfather, Thomas Henry Huxley—who championed Charles Darwin's revolutionary theories—he had the mind and instincts of a scientist. Not by intention, but rather by necessity, Huxley himself added another dimension: spirituality. To acquire knowledge and write well were once all that mattered to Huxley, but after a dazzlingly successful early career, he began to realize that to marshall facts and write elegantly was not enough. There was something far more important in every person's life.

That "something" may have been deep in his subconscious, but it had no part in his early writings.

His clever but darkly pessimistic novels, dissecting as they did the decaying but still perfumed corpses of Vic-

101

torian and Edwardian life and manners, assured Huxley enormous success as a young man. His novels about the free-wheeling Jazz Age effectively satirized the bright, young, hollow people of the era. To college students in the 1920s and 1930s, he was a cult hero, mercilessly pummeling their stultified, decadent society. It was a time when Freud and his followers were burrowing into the subconscious, when Darwin showed that creation was not a Divine act in six days but an evolutionary process of millions of years. The eruptions of this new scientific age shook the pillars of established religious faiths. Huxley at once applauded the scientific revolution and, through his characters, pointed out how foolishly humankind was going about utilizing its benefits. The popular morality that many decent people espoused—but few lived—had never before been so deftly skewered as in Huxley's devastatingly irreverent books.

In works like *Chrome Yellow* and *Antic Hay* he put his ear to the doors of drawing room and bedroom and relayed to his growing readership the inanities of the British upper middle class. He called his time the "Age of Noise" and he brilliantly recorded the cacophony. He didn't hide his disgust for the foibles of mankind; he mocked science and religion, together with this alleged "new man" emerging from the rubble with the arrogance to believe he would chart his own destiny, do anything he chose to do. An entire generation of young readers would point to Huxley as a man who had helped free them from the conventions of the past and encouraged them to look clearly at the fatuousness of their day. And there was equally a generation of parents who considered Aldous Huxley a clear and present danger to

Aldous Huxley

their family, their moral code, and to the future happiness and welfare of their children.

The writing of the first half of his life culminated in the book that leapt from the arrogance of the day to the not-too-distant future in which man's planned universe was a reality, a "Brave New World" where fetuses were raised in test tubes; in which human drones and superior beings were created in exact numbers according to society's need for them; where unhappiness was quickly cured by ingesting the proper drug; where the exercise of free will and romantic love were considered threats to the good of society.

His novel of a Utopian dream gone awry would forever have a place on the list of seminal books. Aldous Huxley had put man in his place, effectively squashing this bug that had come up from the primeval slime. He had reflected the intellectual and moral conflicts of the collective soul of the early 20th century and had forecast (with painful accuracy, as our own current dilemmas with genetic engineering and *in vitro* fertilization so well demonstrate) their effects on future generations.

But even though he was an international celebrity, Huxley was far from a contented man. The human condition that he had so mercilessly described was beginning to haunt him. If he were to be cast as one of the characters in his novels, he would not be, as many people might expect, urbane and smug, but the marginal man—every book contained at least one—who seemed always on the edge of the action, pensive, troubled, ultimately unable to act. In real life, Huxley was an extremely gentle and kind man, but with an intellectual integrity that never allowed him to remain at ease with

103

illusions. He had been trying in his early works to chart accurately the winds of his time, but he was reaching a point in his life when that was no longer enough.

Forty volumes of short stories, fiction, reportage, criticism and essays that Huxley wrote progressed from one extreme to another, divided not by some divine intervention or blinding insight, but by a realization that came slowly and then overtook him: it was not enough to chronicle man and woman's foolishness, no matter how astutely. Ideas were important but it was conduct —the way that people would then live their lives—that had to be changed so that the destructive cycle would stop. The writer's responsibility went beyond producing good books. If people read his words and were not somehow changed for the better, he was a failure.

Pivotal at this point in Huxley's life was his meeting two men. Gerald Heard, science editor of the BBC, was a man with an intellect as vigorous and knowledge as wide-ranging as Huxley's, but with a spiritual view of life that did not deny science and in fact embraced and went beyond it. Krishnamurti, a holy man from India, struck Huxley as a man who not only spoke wise words, but lived them. The pain of his own early life (in which Huxley was blinded for a period with glaucoma), the suicide of his brother when he was still a young man, the desolation of World War I, the fecklessness of the Jazz Age and the giddiness of the 1930s, all weighed upon him. There was more to life than daily triumphs and failures; there *had* to be.

Gradually, like those few literary men and women who forge success into heroism, who risk the derision of an oft-times fickle public accustomed to the facile destruc-

tion and not the arduous and unremittingly demanding
re-constitution of mankind, Huxley began to change
from a successful man of letters to a seeker after the
truth.

Although he lived and died a man of no professed religious belief, Huxley knew that there was a spiritual reality beneath the phenomenal world and he wanted to explore and write about it. He had to be redeemed
somehow, just as man had to be saved from himself.

The second part of his writing life was spent largely in
America, and oddly enough a good deal of it in Holly-
wood, a place not exactly known as a center for transcendence. While he was a sought-after and highly-paid
script writer, Huxley's best efforts appeared in print and
not on the screen. The film "A Woman's Vengeance,"
may not be remembered, but *After Many a Summer
Dies the Swan* will remain one of the most astute fictional commentaries on life and morality in mid-century
America. But perhaps the book that comes closest to
mirroring his own conflicts is *Grey Eminence*. Here
Huxley introduces the reader to Father Joseph, an
ostensibly saintly Capuchin monk hovering so close to
the divine enlightenment he'd sought for a lifetime, yet
unable to achieve the total disinterestedness that con-
stitutes true holiness. Father Joseph serves both God
and Cardinal Richelieu, rationalizing that dedication to
France is akin to fealty to Heaven. His policies help to
extend the Thirty Years' War; famine, disease and can-
nibalism are rampantly spread—all for the good of the
empire. Huxley's message was clear: the best of intentions corrupted by misguided loyalties produce unspeakable sins.

Meanwhile, in his personal life, Huxley struggled to reconcile that spiritual part of himself with the shell that encased him. His senses were alive, his intellect superior; yet he was constantly haunted that these externals betrayed and concealed true reality. As he told his friend Christopher Isherwood, "I have mainly lived in the world of intellectual life and art. But the world of knowing-about-things is unsatisfactory. It's no good knowing about the taste of strawberries out of a book."

His first fans, who relished his agnostic, worldly early books and resonated to the meaninglessness of life they portrayed, were astonished by the Huxley they saw in his new works. Some thought he had gone soft in the head to be treating morality and spirituality so seriously. But there were others who had reached the same point of realizing that such nihilism was a dead end street. They could understand what he was after. "To see this kind of change in a man you idolized couldn't just be dismissed," said Marvin Barrett, who was then a Harvard student. Barrett would later, as a magazine editor, commission the last article Huxley wrote, a consideration of Shakespeare and religion. "People of my generation either parted company with him in horror or had to find out what was there was in the direction he had taken."

Books in his new vein were not greeted with the enthusiasm that had welcomed his early novels and *Brave New World* but rather with indignation and contempt. Undaunted, Huxley forged on. *Ends and Means,* which immediately preceded World War II, was a frontal attack on a time notoriously out of joint, and after it Huxley was ready to go deeper. He launched into an exhaustive search of the philosophies that down through

106

Aldous Huxley

the ages had not merely nourished man's mind, but fed his soul. With his wide-ranging mind, his eclectic tastes, his hunger to find answers to the questions his own heart whispered, he searched for the highest common factors in all religious traditions. In *The Perennial Philosophy,* Huxley combined Taoism, Meister Eckhardt, William Law, Christ and a rich potpourri of religious beliefs and practices into what he called "the nature of ultimate reality." He dramatically illustrated, at a time when West understood little about East and the word "ecumenism" was hardly known, that mysticism filled a universal need of the human soul which knew no national or religious boundaries. He showed that mystics, often with no knowledge of other religious beliefs, had apparently identical visions and ecstasies.

But the taste of strawberries still eluded him. He could write about religious experience, understand it, but somehow he could not abandon ego and reason, could not make the leap of faith required of anyone who wants communion with the Divine. He articulated transcendence, but he could not *feel* it. He desperately wanted that. Hoping that mind-altering drugs might dilate his soul, Huxley, in the days when LSD were so many garbled letters of the alphabet and the name mescaline might be mistaken as a cold remedy or eye drops, experimented with both.

His romance with drugs alienated and confused still more people and confirmed to those who thought he'd gone off the deep end years before that their initial judgment was correct. But Huxley had neither the temperament nor the time to respond to his critics. The end of human life was the direct, intuitive awareness of God—

there could be no other goal, he had finally concluded—and whatever means were available, they should and must be used.

He died of cancer on November 22, 1963, his passing all but unnoticed as the world mourned President John F. Kennedy, assassinated the same day. The dichotomy Huxley had tried to reconcile—the outer existence of man and his inner hunger to transcend himself—had still not been resolved. At the end, the inner Huxley was still on his pilgrimage, his religious yearnings never fully realized. How is it, we might wonder, that a man with such uncommon intelligence and such sincere intention could end up this way? Even with his luminous mind and insatiable curiosity, he was neither able to shape his beliefs into some formula nor accept any one religion or system of belief. If Aldous Huxley couldn't find his peace on earth, was not given the taste of strawberry he so fervently sought, the ordinary seeker might wonder: what hope is there?

Although he continually sought a sublime endpoint, Huxley's consolation was that he equally believed the final integration is less a state one achieves than a continuing dynamic process where the goal might be well understood but never fully realized. If one continues to open his or her eyes to the spirit, there is always more to see, he discovered. Frustration is a given. But so is hope. And Huxley never lost hope. His earthly sight may have been poor, but he was not a man to accept anything less than a complete vision. He went to his grave unfulfilled, but unwavering in his quest.

When the article on which Huxley was working at his death was published, it contained a familiar line from

108

Aldous Huxley

Tennyson that might well serve as the theme and testament to his life. "There lives more faith in honest doubt, believe me, than in half the creeds."

———

Bedford, Sybille, *Aldous Huxley, A Biography,* Harper & Row, New York, 1974.

Birnbaum, Milton, *Aldous Huxley's Search for Values,* Knoxville, U. of Tennessee, 1971.

Huxley, Aldous, *After Many a Summer Dies the Swan,* Harper & Brothers, New York, 1939.

_____, *Brave New World,* Doubleday, New York, 1932.

_____, *Grey Eminence,* Harper & Brothers, New York, 1941.

_____, *The Perennial Philosophy,* Harper & Brothers, New York, 1945.

Huxley, Julian, ed., *Aldous Huxley, A Memorial Volume,* New York, Harper & Row, 1965.

Huxley, Laura Archera, *The Timeless Moment: A Personal View of Aldous Huxley,* New York, Farrar, Straus & Giroux, 1968.

Watts, Harold H., *Aldous Huxley,* Boston, Twayne, 1969.

III. Living on the Edge

Charles de Foucauld

Nikos Kazantzakis

Flannery O'Connor

Rumi

Charles de Foucauld

He was born a Christian, became an agnostic, posed as a rabbi, was converted by Islam, became a monk, priest and hermit, lived in the most God-forsaken part of the world, tried to found a religious order—and died without a follower. But Charles de Foucauld left something behind that would not die.

"I LIVED without a faith; nothing actually seemed to have any certainty about it. The very credulity with which the world pursued a thousand different religions seemed a good enough argument for me to renounce them all."

Many a young person has come to the same conclusion as Charles de Foucauld. Once the pious religious creeds taught in the protected milieu of family and school face off against the conflicting ideologies of the real world and the cruelties meted out by the supposedly righteous, not a

113

few of the once-faithful find that unbelief is more valid than belief.

The Viscount de Foucauld—Charles' formal title—was a highly intelligent (though underachieving) student, rich, overweight and overindulged. He became more taken with the skepticism popularized by Nietzsche, Marx and Rimbaud than he was by the precepts of the Christian faith in which he and his young friends were instructed in the France of the 1860s and 1870s.

He came from an illustrious family of soldiers and statesmen that could trace its ancestors to the 10th century. His was a proud legacy; indeed, the de Foucauld family crest proclaimed *Jamais arriere*—Never retreat.

But Charles was hardly inflamed by such a legacy. His passions and advances lay elsewhere. He liked fine champagne and *pate de foie gras,* all-night parties and friends who shared his zest for the good—albeit dissolute —life. He was a bit of legend in his own time. The mention of the name Viscount de Foucauld in Paris or Pont-a-Mousson or Saumur, places where he went to school, was sure to raise an eyebrow or recall a story of some outrageous drinking bout, gluttonous feast or deflowered maiden.

Unsure of what he wanted for a career, Charles enrolled in the prestigious St. Cyr Military School—France's West Point—and though he experienced fits of discipline and determination to change his life, he eventually graduated near the bottom of his class, still fat and flabby, pages of demerits on his record. When he was posted to Algeria, he sent his mistress ahead to prepare an appropriate apartment for them. Mimi was instructed to introduce herself as the Viscountess and was well received until Charles' regiment arrived and the truth was out. He was given the choice of sending Mimi back to France or banishment from the French army. Charles was soon a civilian.

Some months later, his regiment was pressed into combat to put down a revolt by a powerful sheik, Uled Sidi, and Charles begged to be reinstated so he could serve with them. His wish was granted and, given a direct challenge, Charles amazingly proved to be an excellent and brave officer. "This educated dilettante showed himself . . . capable of undergoing the severest trials," one of his comrades reported.

He fought the rebellious Arabs—the current enemy of his powerful colonial nation—with a soldier's zeal, but while most men in his regiment saw the Arabs as little more than savage pagans and the desert as a wasteland, Charles was struck with both the people and their land. These fierce Moslem warriors bowed so solemnly in prayer five times a day; their bleak landscape had a purity about it that Charles couldn't rid from his mind.

The conflict over, Charles sought not the comfort and security afforded by an Army fort, but rather to be back in the harsh desert. He wanted to explore vast stretches of North Africa that were then uncharted territory. As a Frenchman he knew he would be regarded as a spy and could easily be killed; his knowledge of Islam was too limited for him to pass as a Moslem. So he arranged to travel as a Jewish rabbi with another rabbi, the old man Mardochee, who was an experienced desert voyager.

In nine months Charles covered almost 2,000 miles, taking readings along the way and charting an area of Morocco whose villages, cities and terrain were heretofore unknown to mapmakers. He was celebrated on his return, but the journey had produced more than accurate longitudes, latitudes and altitudes. He had encountered Jews living in unspeakable conditions, forced into ghettos, but practicing a faith that had survived persecution and suffering for thousands of years. And again he encountered the solemnity and spirituality of the Moslems. In time, he would write, "Islam was responsible for a profound change in me . . . My exposure to this faith, and to these souls living always in God's presence, helped me to understand that there is something greater and more real than the pleasures of this world."

As so many who had found their souls stirred by the vast bleakness and silent loneliness of the desert, by the inner strength of desert people, something was happening within Charles de Foucauld.

He returned time and again to North Africa, until he had explored from Tangier to Tunis; he almost married; he spent time in France, in Switzerland; there were days-long orgies and weeks of remorse. Charles was restless; something inside him was urging him on, but to where, for what? He told his cousin Marie, "You are a happy believer, but when I search for the light, I do not find it." Like Thomas Merton, whose conversion began with a visit to a tiny church in the midst of New York City, Charles began to haunt the church of St. Augustine in Paris. He walked the aisles, mumbling over and over again to himself, "My God, if you exist, make your existence known to me." At St. Augustine, he met the Abbe Huvelin, the man who would begin the shaping of a new Charles de Foucauld.

Charles de Foucauld

At the Abbe's recommendation, he traveled to the Holy Land and there, sporting a fine handlebar moustache and clothes of Parisian cut—hardly the image of the seeking pilgrim—he trod the ancient streets and visited the places where Jesus' life unfolded. Surprisingly for a man so used to ostentation, he found it was not the public life of Jesus that attracted him, but rather the 30 years He spent in Nazareth, unknown to the outside world. "Little"—the word little— kept welling up within him.

As he searched for direction, those ageless words from both the Old and New Testament pointed a way: "You shall love the Lord your God with all your heart, and all your soul, and all your mind. And you shall love your neighbor as yourself."

Charles was never a man to do anything half-heartedly anyhow, so once his conversion was underway, he knew he wanted nothing less than a total commitment. He joined the Trappists and—dressed in a shabby, torn white habit, eating a meager diet and spending hours in prayer and manual labor—he spent the next seven years of his life trying to "Vanish before God into pure nothingness."

Although he already was a member of one of the most austere religious orders in the world, and was living at one of its most impoverished houses, he wanted a still simpler, poorer life. After being sent to a Trappist monastery in Syria he was asked to sit vigil with the body of an Arab who had worked for the Catholics of the area, and there he saw clearly what he must do. In this home, the poverty of the Trappists looked like luxury. They had security in numbers, a world-wide network, land, benefactors; this poor Arab had nothing but what he had earned each day. De Foucauld was protected; the poor Arabs had no such security and as warring factions rose up against each other, there often was no sanctuary, no escape.

Charles had to live like them. In every way. He had to leave the safety of a religious order behind, the comforts of a monastery, the continuity of a tradition. If he was to live out the mandate to love completely, he had to abandon himself—not only looking after the poor and the outcast, but to living with them, like them.

No religious order at the time had set itself such a task, so de Foucauld dreamed of founding one that would. He would call it the Congregation of the Little Brothers of Jesus. These Little Brothers would live in small communities in dwellings like those of the very poorest people. According to the rule that de Foucauld began to write, they would earn their livelihood at menial work, accept no donations, share everything, welcoming everyone and offering whatever food or shelter they had. At the end of the week, when they were paid, if any money was left over from the week before, it would immediately be distributed to the poor. If travel was required, it would be in the lowest class. If the poor walked, they would walk.

De Foucauld sent the proposed rule to Abbe Huvelin. "Do you want me to be honest with you?" he promptly responded. "It frightens me. Go live, by all means, at the outskirts of some community and practice all the humility you care to, but please, I beg of you, don't write any more rules!"

Released by the Trappists, de Foucauld took up resi-

118

dence in a tiny tool shed at the gate of a convent in Nazareth, but his dream persisted to live with "the very sickest of souls, amidst the most abandoned of society." His mind wandered over the landscapes he knew so well. Africa! In the Moroccan interior, an area as large as France itself, there were ten million people and not a single priest. De Foucauld had fought being ordained, feeling he was not worthy of the priesthood, but now he saw the good that could come from what to him was a painful decision to obey the bidding of his Trappist superior.

Father de Foucauld eventually settled in an oasis in the Saoura region in Southern Morocco called Beni-Abbes. There was an army outpost there, but the population was preponderantly *haratins,* black Moslems who survived on a meager diet of dates and millet and were constantly under threat from any of a long list of marauders who not only periodically plundered their fields, but also took them as slaves.

Except for the small wooden cross on the thatched palm frond roof, his home was no different than the other Arab huts around Beni-Abbes. He built five small rooms—one for himself, two for guests and two for the co-workers he hoped would soon join him—and a tiny chapel. He said Mass, tended a garden and began work on "The Gospel for Poor Negroes of the Sahara" should any of them come to him for more than food and shelter. He received whoever came to him, with whatever need. Soldiers from the fort, their commandant, Moslems, Jews, slaves—both freed and in bondage—came to his simple home. For the slave, the need might be bread and shelter; for the soldier away from home, friendship and a good book; for the illiterate, a letter written; for a family in conflict, advice.

The poor admired him, for he lived even poorer than they. Yet when he was invited to eat with the officers, only the most observant among them were aware of the extreme asceticism he practiced. For de Foucauld never flaunted the privations he subjected himself to; when dishes were passed, he took some of everything. His charming, amusing conversation covered the reality that he actually ate very little. He took ill more than once, and on one occasion was diagnosed with scurvy.

And year after year, while his rooms filled with those needing shelter, no one came to work with him. He could claim no converts.

De Foucauld was, of course, a believing and ardent Catholic, a priest, but it's important to realize he didn't go to the desert as a missionary. "I want to accustom everyone—Christian, Moslem, Jew or pagan—to look on me as a brother, a universal brother" he wrote. "They are beginning to call the house 'the brotherhood,' (*khaoua* in Arabic) and that is sweet to my ears."

De Foucauld embraced the most basic principle that the Jesus whose footsteps he followed in Nazareth had proclaimed. All men and women were creatures of God; none was more worthy because of choice of religion or place in the world. All were equally deserving of love.

De Foucauld was a prodigious writer and correspondent, so much of what he saw and thought survives him. His view of the desert is particularly poignant: "To receive the grace of God," he wrote a fellow Trappist, "you must go to a desert place and stay awhile. There you can be emptied and unburdened of everything that does not pertain to God. There the house of your soul is swept clean to make room for God alone to dwell. The Israelites had to pass through the desert. Moses lived there before he was commissioned for his lifework. St. Paul, St. John Chrysostom—both of them served apprenticeship in the desert. . . . We need this silence, this absence of every creature, so that God can build his hermitage within us."

He considered his small hut his hermitage and it was only on rare and needed occasions that he ventured out; he stayed put and welcomed others in.

Although he was a hermit, he knew from his many visitors and mail exactly what was happening in the Sahara, Africa, France and the world. After he had been at Beni-Abbes but a few years, he heard of new violence to the west, an area in Morocco called El Hoggar, at the very center of the arid Sahara. There, amidst some of the most unforgiving land on the face of the earth lived the legendary Touareg, fierce warriors of the desert, camel riders of extraordinary skill, merciless when they descended on a caravan, blue veils covering their faces. Tribal warfare was sweeping El Hoggar and France was ready to make the best of the instability to expand its colonial empire.

A letter from an old St. Cyr classmate, stationed on the border of El Hoggar, stirred something in de Foucauld. He had thought he would spend his life in Beni-Abbes, but suddenly he knew he had to leave.

De Foucauld set out for El Hoggar and, while he often traveled in camel caravans, walked most of the time. In ten months he covered over 3,000 miles, virtually all on foot. He wandered through the bleak canyons and gazed at the ancient eruptions of lava that thrust jagged volcanic peaks thousands of feet into the air. He talked to the Touareg as best he could and each day studied more of their language. He shared whatever he had with these nomads, aware that as a Frenchman he was immediately suspect, a spy; as a Christian, an infidel.

A fateful meeting with the powerful chieftain Amenokal Moussa led to de Foucauld's new home. De Foucauld told him that he wanted to learn the Touareg language and live with the people. Others might have laughed, but when Moussa looked at this man with the burning, dark eyes something told him this was someone he could trust and believe. De Foucauld settled at Tamranrasset, a bleak settlement of some 20 families. There he built himself a hut of reeds and a chapel, nine feet long and five feet wide, covering it with the branches of scrubs.

There was something at once magnetic and confusing about the *"marabout* of the red heart" as he was known, because of the heart and cross emblem he wore on his coarse garment. He was white, he was unarmed. He had placed himself in their midst, at their mercy. He gave alms instead of asking for them.

He spent the next 13 years with the Touareg, meeting their needs as they arose: from instructing the Amenokal on the intricacies of the colonial mind, something the leader could not fathom, to collecting Touareg poetry and proverbs and even writing a grammar for the language. Drought and famine came as they always had, but Father de Foucauld was now among them, gathering the children each day for what might be their only meal. He begged medicines and cured people. They came to love him; once, when he was severely ill during a drought, they set their own misery aside and brought him food and goat milk that saved his life.

His was a church without borders, a love without boundaries or preconditions. He saw clearly that what passed as civility or civilization in his native France —that cradle of Catholicism—was no more than the masquerade of a people supposedly more developed than the Touareg in their tents of animal hides and mud huts. He wrote, "If we treat them like savages they will treat us like savages."

In 1916, tribal warfare again rumbled across the desert; the Senoussistes, a tribe from Tripoli, had revolted and had already attacked a French fort. But de Foucauld would not hear of leaving his people. On the night of December 1, after a knock on his door, he called out. The answer was a familiar voice, a *haratin* to whom he'd given shelter and food. De Foucauld opened the door. Behind the man were twenty others, Senoussistes sure that the priest and his tiny compound were ripe for plunder. A young Senoussiste was left to guard de Foucauld and when the sound of other camel riders sounded in the distance, he panicked.

A single shot through the head ended the life of Charles de Foucauld.

Charles de Foucauld left no disciples; his "fraternities" never came into being during his lifetime. But he left behind something else that would not die with his body: an idea, an ideal—one so simple and strong. It took some 20 years, but an order of men, the Little Brothers of Jesus, and then one of women, the Little Sisters of Jesus, were eventually begun. (Three others

would eventually be founded, based on his example.)
Remembering the words of de Foucauld about manual
labor—"What compassion it gives you for the poor,
what love for the laboring man!"—and living in groups
of three or four or five, these Little Brothers and Sisters
share the life and the neighborhoods of the underpriv-
ileged in locations around the world. They may live in a
bamboo hut, a cave or squatter's shack, a gypsy's
wagon, a cheap tenement. Often, when their employers
find that this sweeper or that machine operator is a professed and educated religious, privileges or advancement
will be extended to them—and are always refused. They
wear the clothes of the working man and woman, eat
their food, work their shifts, suffer the uncertainties of
layoffs and strikes.

Like their spiritual leader they do not evangelize, but
receive those who come to them and those they work
with in an absolutely disinterested way, a mute—but
powerful—witness to God's love among men and
women. With the Bedouins in the desert, miners in Belgium, the destitute in Washington, D.C. or outside
Rome, these quiet followers of Charles de Foucauld
carry on the legacy of a man who took seriously the
commandment of love.

Carrouges, Michel, *Soldier of the Spirit,* trans. by Marie-
Christine Hellin, G.P. Putnam's Sons, New York, 1956.

De Foucauld, Charles, *Meditations of a Hermit,* trans. by
Charlotte Balfour, Orbis Books, New York, reissued 1981.

Freemantle, Anne, *Desert Calling,* Holt, New York, 1949.

Charles de Foucauld

Lorit, Sergius C., *Charles de Foucauld, the Silent Witness,* trans. by Ted Morrow, New York Press, Jamaica, New York, 1966.

Six, Jean-Francois, *Witness in the Desert,* trans. by Lucie Noel, Macmillan, New York, 1965.

Nikos Kazantzakis

Passion. How often have we been told it was something to either avoid all together or keep tightly in check. Nikos Kazantzakis would hear of no such thing as he plummeted through life in his quest to live—and to tell.

IN A cemetery high above the Aegean Sea at Heraklion, on a craggy knoll studded with the rocks that have been for centuries the bane of the hearty people of Crete, stands a simple wooden cross. "I have nothing . . . I fear nothing . . . I am free," reads the epitaph below the name Nikos Kazantzakis.

He was born in this unpretentious capital city in 1885 and, in 1957, laid to rest. But Kazantzakis was seldom here in the years between, for he was a restless man on a personal odyssey, relentlessly seeking to reconcile his passionate love of sensuous existence—the things of this earth—with the hunger of his spiritual yearnings. Kazantzakis knew well that both existed in every man and woman and, to be fully human, each had to be ardently pursued. To Kazantzakis, there was no greater sin than

126

Nikos Kazantzakis

to suppress one's humanity in hopes of becoming more spiritual—except, perhaps, to ignore the spiritual self and embrace the ways of the world completely.

His life is a testimony to that quest, a cornucopia of experiences, of travels through many distant lands and a diverse sampling of philosophies. During one richly variegated period, communism and Christianity both made ultimate sense to Kazantzakis—and also repelled him. He pronounced that he could think of only two people who deserved to be alive on this wretched planet, two men rarely mentioned in the same breath: Christ and Lenin. He wrote plays, poetry, fiction, literary history, journalism, political and ethical polemics, travel books; translated Greek classics and children's books; performed 30 years of government service; and worked on encyclopedias and dictionaries. Fiercely in love with both God and Greece, his rewards were to be exiled by his homeland, excoriated by the Vatican and ultimately to have one of his books—one with a religious theme at that—placed on the Index of Forbidden Books. Early in his career he was hauled into court and accused of trying to destroy religion, morality and Greece! Not only did the Greek Orthodox hierarchy condemn him in his lifetime, but in death, it denied Kazantzakis a church burial.

Ah, Nikos, what a Companion you are! When any of us feel unappreciated, we can turn to you, who made misunderstanding a fine art.

It's fitting that he is buried at Heraklion, where he can easily look in all directions. The visitor to Kazantzakis' grave—at this ancient crossroads between East and West—can almost sense the impatient, indefatig-

127

able old Greek sniffing the wind, looking first out to sea, then behind him to the land and people he loved so dearly, wondering what direction he should go today.

Standing on the rocky cliff it's easy to imagine him, like Zorba the Greek (the character for whom he is best known), tossing back his head and howling with laughter at how the world treated and regarded him. And like Zorba, with a wrinkle of a smile still on his face, with no trace of malice in his heart, his pockets empty and his heart pounding with excitement and anticipation, he's ready to leap once more into life.

His outpouring of writing was prodigious, torrential, varied and uneven. He was out of favor and condemned more often than he was praised or even accepted. But regardless of the public's fancy, there was only one goal he pursued throughout his life.

The major and almost the only theme of all my work is the struggle of man with 'God': the unyielding, inextinguishable struggle of the naked worms called 'man' against the terrifying power and darkness of the forces within him and around him. The stubbornness of the struggle, the tenacity of the little spark in its fight to penetrate the age-old, boundless night and conquer it. The anguished battle to transmute darkness into light, slavery into freedom. . . .

When Kazantzakis is read today, it is not to discover a fine literary craftsman adept at plotting or realism or characterization. It is to listen to a man driven to write about the human condition, a prophet who cannot temper the urgency of his words, a human being so overwhelmed with the beauty and inequity of life that he must constantly record what he has discovered.

He called himself at turns a pessimist and a tragic optimist, an atheist who wanted to live in a monastery, but first and foremost, Kazantzakis was a "promoter of 'man, the creator of God.'" Like many philosophers and holy men before him, he believed in an impossible dream: the perfectability of those "naked worms." His life was dedicated to an adage that at first might be construed as vain or selfish: "Create an idolized image of yourself, and try to resemble it." But, to Kazantzakis, this was a credo as selfless, God-seeking and holy as any intoned in church. It was his own unique recipe for sainthood.

He never flinched from the realization that the considered life was any other than a series of conflicts. He loved to quote an Indian apothegm in which the seeker asks, "What is the right path?"

"The path of God," is the answer.

"And what is the path of God?" the seeker persists.

"The uphill path."

Kazantzakis tilted at windmills like Don Quixote and again and again pushed the stone up the mountain like Sisyphus, but he was sure that it was the only way to live a life. He constantly wrestled with his heart to make it obey the exigencies of his soul. "I've learned one thing: that man can still make the miracle descend upon the earth," he told his wife, Eleni. "It's enough if he avoids the highway leading to easy happiness and chooses the uphill path leading to the impossible."

Companions Along the Way

Many people today complain of the complexity and unsettledness of our day, but Kazantzakis reveled in the knowledge that he had been born into a "transitional age." In the early part of our century, as he looked around him, it was apparent that man had already lost his appreciation of this world's beauty, lost his simple faith in the heavens above and frankly didn't know which way to turn or what to believe in. But Kazantzakis was not a man to throw up his arms in exasperation or piously turn inward, waiting for history to settle out. Confusion! Turmoil! What opportunity!

Kazantzakis saw the struggle of modern "transitional" man as the *very path to salvation*. Love all things, but stick to none, he advised. It was his conviction that the striving on the part of every individual to integrate the seemingly polarized desires for the things of this life with the hunger for God was a prelude to Union with the One. Man the animal struggles with man the spirit, so that man can eventually rest in the Pure Spirit.

At times he despaired, both with himself and the "worms" about him, but there was a unmistakable stubbornness about Kazantzakis' vision, a steadfast refusal to capitulate. It was a mixed blessing, both for Kazantzakis and those who knew him. In a dream, Kazantzakis hears a fellow Cretan talking to him:

> What we feel for you is hatred and love. We say bad things about you. We consider you a monster. We don't want to talk with you. All your actions seem somber to us, full of egoism and cruelty. But the moment you appear, the whole rhythm changes: You seem to us full of love. We see sacrifices in all

130

Nikos Kazantzakis

your acts; an exemplary struggle in your whole life.
When you leave, we see the same darkness again.

A journalist friend was more succinct:

I didn't want to come to see you. You are my conscience and I prefer not to hear it.

He was a strange amalgam of a man, this Nikos Kazantzakis. He was tall and angular, with piercing black eyes, and wore his poorly tailored suits with baronial elegance. He always carried an immaculately clean pair of white gloves. He wanted money and luxury, because they would afford him the ability to work more freely, but on his travels, he often rode with the peasants in fourth class coaches. Whenever he had the amenities he coveted, he was immediately troubled. He felt the person seeking comfort had already allowed the devil to make a down payment on his soul. He constantly bemoaned the fact that his travels separated him from his beloved Eleni, but after a tearful reunion, he'd be making plans for his next trip. He felt his life was one constant discovery, and that to rest or be satisfied that he had seen enough or done enough to make the world a better place would be to admit defeat.

Each year he designated his birthday, February 18, as a day of recollection. And each year, though he might have produced more books, plays and translations than some people accomplish in twenty years, he concluded he had squandered his talents. But then? In typical Zorba style, Kazantzakis would leap into the next work, convinced *this time* he would write something meaningful.

... I rejoice that there have been a few spirits who have felt a little joy in reading what I've tried to save of my own soul—by dint of great effort, by giving flesh to it in words. I desire no other reward. There can be no greater reward for a hermit.

His zest for life was boundless; he had but few regrets and only two requests. He wanted ten arms and twelve disciples so that he could accomplish all the projects that were buzzing around in his brain. As might be surmised, he was always a fascinating partner—but not an accommodating husband. In her biography of her beloved *Nikosmou,* his wife Eleni wrote:

I am neither idealizing my companion nor disparaging him. It was not always easy to breathe his fiery air. But if he preferred the bare branch for himself, he never imposed it on others. Between convenient compromise and his own dignity, he never hesitated. He proudly refused the easy chair.

Throughout his life he wrote about man's search for God, but Kazantzakis' ever-changing, never quantifiable God is not one who conveniently fits into any religion's textbook. In *Symposium,* he writes:

Rise up. You seek God? There He is: Action, replete with mistakes, fumblings, persistence, agony. God is not the power that has found eternal equilibrium, but the power that is forever breaking every equilibrium, forever searching for a higher one. Whosoever struggles and makes progress by the same method in his own narrow sphere finds God and works with him. Rise up and go out among human beings. Learn to love them and to kill them—love is respect, affection, loathing.

And then, lest no one be offended (or he be too easily accepted), he goes on, switching into the anti-clerical vein that so enraged the Church.

The enemy is the God dressed in cassock, fingering the rosary, unwashing, unmarried, indolent . . .

In *The Last Temptation of Christ,* the God is Epaphus, the Greek god of "touch," who

. . . Prefers flesh to shadow and like the wolf in the proverb does not wait upon the promises of others when it is a question of filling his belly. . . . The most reliable and industrious of all the gods, who walks the earth, loves the earth, wishes to remake it 'in his own image and after his likeness'—that was my god.

Above all, Kazantzakis' God was the *elan vital,* that pulsating force surging through the universe, part of man as man is part of God, constantly striving to make man purer, better, freer. God was in him, Kazantzakis knew, as he was in God. They were partners, co-workers on earth, chained to one another, bound by love and mutual need and continuing conflict.

In order to find that God, know Him better, understand and come closer to Him, Kazantzakis constantly sought some sure means—a place, a way. He went to Mount Athos and other Greek monasteries, hoping that the ascetic life would somehow purify and compose him. He loved the days spent in silence, eating sparse meals, reading, praying, but each time he came away unsatisfied. He found the monks lacking, somehow deadened by the monastic life, not animated and stimulated by it. "However much I yearn for a harsh, ascetic life, the human heart in me is insatiable," he sadly concluded. At one point in his life, he saw the only answer was to completely reorganize Hellenic asceticism; at another, he was ready to take over a monastery and make it "a workshop of the spirit."

Kazantzakis was obsessed with writing about man's search for goodness in this life and oftentimes his characters seem ill-fated, bound for martyrdom. Because of the beckoning of their inner voices, they are unable to fit in to their time. He reached back into history, passing such classic figures as Odysseus, Dante, Buddha and St. Francis of Assisi through the prism of his own conscience. If they were known as saints, sainthood was quickly stripped from them at Kazantzakis' hands. They fail miserably, despair—but ultimately, like the indomitable Zorba, created by this master himself, they rise again and go on.

His Jesus in *The Last Temptation of Christ* is utterly human, only tangentially divine and, of course, still another literary reflection of Kazantzakis himself, wrestling with repressions and lusts, locked in the conflict between flesh and soul. "Some were shocked that Christ had temptations," he wrote to a friend. "But while I was writing this book, I felt what Christ felt. I became Christ. And I knew definitely that great temptations, extremely enchanting and often legitimate ones, came to hinder him on his road to Golgotha. But how would theologians know this?"

Nikos Kazantzakis

The Catholic Church was not pleased with such a bold interpretation and the book was placed on the Index, forbidden reading for anyone who professed to follow the Christ acceptable to the church. His reply to the Vatican quoted Tertullian, the fiery 2nd century heretic: "In Your courtroom, Lord, I appeal."

Undaunted, and aware his public acceptance was at a new low, Kazantzakis wrote more and more on spiritual themes in the last years of his life: about Christ, St. Francis of Assisi and, in his autobiographical *Report to Greco,* directly about himself. When he knew he was dying, he became possessed with writing as much as he possibly could. Time was running out; he was so far from his goal. God was still so distant. Somehow, he felt he could burn out the disease and finally find God with the intensity of his creative drive. During his final illness, he probably wrote more than when he was in good health. Finally, with a huge bandage covering his infected eye and so weak he couldn't write himself, he dictated to Eleni.

Although Kazantzakis's life saw him move closer and closer to stronger and stronger religious convictions, he was not about to have one of those death bed conversions that would have neatly ended the fascinating story of his life. No, not our Kazantzakis/Zorba. A Protestant pastor and a Catholic priest stood at the bedside, ready to pray with the dying man, to give him the blessings of their respective churches, pluck him from the clutches of the devil who had had far too much sway during his lifetime.

By this time, Kazantzakis was almost blind, but not blind enough not to know who they were and why they were there.

Companions Along the Way

Nikos Kazantzakis turned his face away from them and to the wall. He had talked to God in his own special way throughout his lifetime and now, approaching death, he saw no reason to have intermediaries in this most intimate dialogue.

Kazantzakis, Helen, *Nikos Kazantzakis: A Biography Based on His Letters,* Simon & Schuster, New York, 1968.

Kazantzakis, Nikos, *The Last Temptation of Christ,* Touchstone Books, Simon & Schuster, New York, 1971.

_____, *Report to Greco,* Touchstone Books, Simon & Schuster, New York, 1975.

_____, *Zorba the Greek,* Touchstone Books, Simon & Schuster, New York, 1971.

Flannery
O'Connor

*A vision of the world that
most people around us think
is wacky. An impious
approach to things religious.
Flannery O'Connor was
misunderstood in her day—
and in ours—but she held on
doggedly to what she saw as
holy in the most mundane
and often horrible events.*

F EW WRITERS have been so loved and hated, misunderstood and over-analyzed, lionized and dis-
claimed, reviled and revered as Flannery O'Connor. Her
characters are unforgettable to be sure: rapists, murder-
ers, idiots, armless and legless freaks, the hopeless
young and the desperate old. Violence seethes from the
pages of the two novels and the thirty-odd short stories
that comprise her life's work. Although she claimed hers
was a message of hope and transcendence, tragedy
looms at the turn of almost every page.

And perhaps what equally outrages and confuses her
detractors is that the author was a shy, soft-spoken

137

Companions Along the Way

Southern woman, a semi-invalid who lived quietly with her widowed mother outside the tiny Georgia town of Milledgeville. Certainly Flannery O'Connor could never have known any of the people she wrote about, have heard such coarse talk or been a witness to such horrid actions. Why did she drag mankind through such mud? Was the human race as wretched as she painted them?

But to take at face value Hazel Motes and Manley Pointer, and such irresistibly tantalizing concoctions as Solace Layfield and Sabbath Lily—characters made famous by O'Connor—is to certainly miss what she was after, both in her literature and in her life. At a time that proved to be the dawning of our present age of secular escapism, Flannery O'Connor held up a mirror in front of us—distorted a bit, to be sure—so that we could see what our society and world were becoming and what we were losing as feel-good morality and negotiable ethics were eagerly being received in exchange for an old-fashioned awe of God and the simple belief in good and evil, right and wrong.

It doesn't take a great intellect to see that there's something terribly wrong with a world that idolizes evanescent pop stars, TV preachers with toll free numbers and a pair of jeans with the *au courant* label; something missing in a society running breathlessly to every new fad that claims to reshape body, mind or spirit. Yet when such abuses were still in their infancy, it took a discerning seeress with an enormous talent like Flannery O'Connor's to force us to confront our naked selves in the dehumanizing wilderness created by radical secularity.

Flannery O'Connor saw so clearly that postmodern

138

man and woman were losing their bearings in a world that had begun to worship intellect not spirit, gurus and not God, the secular rather than the sacred, which looked to pop psychology and not theology or morality for the ultimate answers. And she was certain it would take no gentle prodding to wake them from this *acedia*, this sickness of the soul which had insidiously infected so many lives. She wrote:

> When you can assume that your audience holds the same beliefs you do, you can relax a little and use more normal ways of talking to it; when you have to assume that it does not, then you have to make your vision apparent by shock—to the hard of hearing you shout, and for the almost blind you draw large and startling figures.

She died in 1964 at the age of 39, having suffered most extremely painful hereditary blood disease which also claimed her father's life. Except for two years at the University of Iowa and another two years in New York and Connecticut, O'Connor's was a most circumscribed life, certainly dictated by her illness, but concomitantly monastic in its single-minded approach to her writing. Confinement proved not a limitation at all, but a strength.

She was a brilliant student at Georgia State College for Women in Milledgeville and acclaimed at Iowa for her trenchant, unblinking prose. Even at an early age, she was sure of her vision. One of her short stories won a prestigious award and something a young, unknown writer covets—a publisher's option. As the short story was being expanded into what would become her first novel, *Wise Blood,* her editor found the work in progress "bizarre" but allowed he "was willing to work with her" to bring it into shape. O'Connor was outraged. Unpublished, twenty-three years old, she was determined that if she did eventually have a book in print, it would not be what conventional taste dictated. She was not about to be homogenized into another writer who crafted her work according to what was selling in currently popular fiction. Finally, the editor released her from the option, only after calling a woman who would go on to become one of the great writers of mid-century America "stiff-necked, uncooperative and unethical."

The first two appraisals of her nature Flannery O'Connor wouldn't have wasted much time in defending, but "unethical" was certainly another issue. Hers was a life not dedicated to recognition—which came early and multiplied quickly—but to excellence, and a certain kind of excellence. She saw the spiritual darkness in our day and it alarmed her. She wanted, with all the power she could muster, to cast some light. She is an inspiration to any writer who feels he or she has something worthwhile to say—only to find deaf ears and uncomprehending editors—and to seekers who more than occasionally feel they are swimming against the tide of temporal folly.

Flannery O'Connor echoed Hannah Arendt's prescient appraisal of the "banality of evil" in our time. It was apparent to O'Connor that too often the aberrant and distorted came across as natural, as the norm, somehow reasonable. At a minimum, no one was really at *fault.* Evil had become sanitized, acceptable (think of all the books and movies about worthless rogues that have appeared just in the past few years), often perversely heroic; there was always a reason "why" people acted as they did. Their upbringing, a harsh word, poor economic conditions or schooling had warped them—and therefore they were to be absolved of accountability for their actions.

O'Connor saw it as her life's work to cut through this "haze of compassion," not to allow our perception of what was good and decent and what was plainly wrong to be lost any further in the swirling clouds of secular humanism. In her writing, her criminals soundly reject any psycho-social explanations for their actions. Rufus Florida Johnson of "The Lame Shall Enter First" attributes his evil ways to none other than the Devil. Manley Pointer of "Good Country People" acts as he does because he believes in nothing and never has.

Faith—and plainly the lack of it—is a recurring theme in O'Connor's work. Her world is bleak and loveless because there is no touchstone. Without faith as a guide for intellect, truth and error seem equally reasonable. But onto this arid wasteland, O'Connor sprinkles humor —people are so evil, the situations so bleak, that you can do little but laugh at such hyperrealism—and highlights the gnawing, oftentimes begrudging search for redemption. After all, her characters are so low and detestable that they *need* to be saved. In each of her works, there comes the moment when her sinners are aware of the awful unavoidability of grace. If they only can face themselves for what they are, accept their true selves, they can have a new life. O'Connor was obsessed with wholeness, the ways it is broken by stubbornness and stupidity and how it can possibly be restored.

Companions Along the Way

Individual accountability—a rather dusty and equally stiff-necked concept—was what she pounded home time and again. A person is always free to choose between good and evil; make your choice and reap the results.

Readers—even those who applaud her prophetic vision —often wonder about O'Connor: Why was her view so unremittingly squalid? why did a woman of her superior capacities have to drag readers back and forth across so bleak a terrain? She and the avant garde writers of the 1950s and 1960s—a time when America was smugly patting itself on the back—were often assailed for downgrading rather than uplifting American values during this era of national triumphalism. She had a ready response:

> . . . the writer who emphasizes spiritual values is very likely to take the darkest view of all of what he sees in this country today. For him, the fact that we are the most powerful and the wealthiest nation in the world doesn't mean a thing in any positive sense. The sharper the light of faith, the more glaring are apt to be the distortions the writer sees in the life around him.

Like an Old Testament prophet, Flannery O'Connor spoke not in muted tones but in a clear and resounding voice, using allegory and metaphor, weaving modern day parables to make her points. If parting the Red Sea so that the Israelites might escape and their enemies drown can be taken as a providential, geological sleight of God's hand, so might Hazel Motes blinding himself in desperation be the work of a mad anti-Christ. But no, that's not all there is to either tale. As Motes awaits his death—and salvation—in darkness, we are witness to the birth of a primitive Protestant saint.

O'Connor leaves her characters with us to haunt and prod and offend—and ultimately instruct us about our petty conflicts, falsities, obsessions, vanities. "Didn't I turn away from . . . ?", we find ourselves asking. "Didn't I tell him that . . . ?" "Didn't I promise myself I would never again . . . ?" Her stories are so many chapters of an apocalypse; we are left to write our own postlude.

To face O'Connor's characters is to confront some of our many faces. Or—as Flannery O'Connor felt so deeply—to face Truth, the living God. But this is to be no walk along the beach, hearing the warm breeze as the murmurs of God's voice, or a visit with a cozy old friend; instead, as one of her eulogists said, it is ". . . a terrifying vision, to be faced only by the stout of heart."

For her self-imposed campaign to help right the human race, O'Connor was chastised by Catholics who suspected she was at a minimum lapsed, probably a heretic, and possibly an atheist, and by Protestants who felt she was mocking them, as most of her characters are Bible-belt fundamentalists. Few of them knew her library at Milledgeville was filled with books by the finest theologians, mystics and spiritual writers. She grounded herself in de Chardin and Rahner and Aquinas, Heidegger, Buber and St. Teresa of Avila. She knew Scripture as well as most scholars.

As a devout and practicing Catholic, she felt a deep desire to communicate a vision of a hopeful life. But each morning, as she spent the three hours writing that took her the rest of the day to recover from, the hound of heaven chased her characters across the page, the devil embraced them tenderly, the world gave them no simple answers. And they marched on to their deserved fate as God loomed in the background, waiting patiently, watching their foolishness.

Fifteen years after her death, when her work was the subject of far too many theses, term papers, articles and books, a collection of Flannery O'Connor's letters was published. She had always admired works that recorded the inner journey, the adventures of the soul, but concluded she personally could never write one. She had nothing to say about her own inner life, no gospel to preach, no special wisdom to proclaim, no message to impart. She would have been surprised indeed to know that through her letters, she had written a most unique and compelling portrait of an artist's soul.

The Habit of Being is the collection's title and the Flannery O'Connor who emerges from its pages is a remarkably humble, funny, self-deprecating, insightful and intensely spiritual woman. As her dear friend Sally Fitzgerald notes in the introduction:

> Flannery consciously sought to attain to the habit of art [a term she'd learned from Jacques Maritain's *Art and Scholasticism*] and did, by customary exercise and use, acquire it in the making of her novels and stories. Less deliberately perhaps, and only in the course of living in accordance with her formative beliefs, as she consciously and profoundly wished to do, she acquired as well, I think, a second distinguished habit, which I have called 'the habit of being': an excellence not only

of action but of interior disposition and activity that increasingly reflected the object, the being, which specified it, and was itself reflected in what she did and said.

Her illness, which struck O'Connor in her prime and plagued her for fifteen of her thirty-nine years, could have made her self-pitying, self-centered. She was neither. As she showed her characters no pity, she accorded herself none either. She responded to hundreds of letters, critiqued countless manuscripts from struggling, unknown writers; she gave moral and spiritual support to any who asked it of her.

Her confinement could have stifled her—she'd wanted to escape the orthodoxy of the South—but it freed her instead. Going back to Milledgeville proved the real beginning of her immersion into the area and its people, not an end. She gave her full attention to the visible world around her and the spiritual life that permeated it. She immersed herself so deeply in her part of the South that she could reproduce its authentic voice.

Her Catholic faith—in those days a religion overladen with dogma, caveat and admonition—could have bound her, limited her vision and made her yet another mediocre apologist. Instead, her faith was her intellectual and spiritual taproot.

Her talent could have made her arrogant—it never did. Her short stories rarely appeared in glossy magazines, her infrequent lectures were to audiences at small Southern or Catholic schools. She did absolutely nothing to nurture her public image. And, although she would not be "worked with," she always listened to advice and rewrote according to the reactions of trusted friends. Flannery O'Connor knew that she could craft a sentence as few writers were able, create unforgettable characters, recreate dialogue that rang so true, but this "stiff-necked" woman believed her special gifts were on loan from a Power higher than she, a benevolence to be used well during her days on earth. Her intellect was hers to employ and enjoy, but it was only one element in her life, not a god to be adored.

It must have been a continuing struggle to rein in her pride—for she was fiercely independent and proud—and not to abuse the powers she had. How difficult not to abandon her faith in a God who others might contend had treated her poorly. Flannery O'Connor's faith was unshakable, but it was hardly always a comfort. She claimed she wasn't capable of mediative prayer because her mind wandered too much. "My prayers are unfeeling, but habitual, not to say dogged."

She summed up her inner life this way:

> When I ask myself how I know I believe, I have no satisfactory answer at all, no assurance at all, no feeling at all . . . all I can say about love of God is, Lord help me in my lack of it. I distrust pious phrases, particularly when they issue from my mouth.

She wasn't sentimental about her faith, her work, herself. There was an honesty about Flannery O'Connor, this "habit of being" forged throughout a life filled with uncommon acclaim and a brutally debilitating illness. When she wrote, her characters were etched with a diamond's point; when she drew a portrait of herself at a particularly bad time in her illness, she painted who she was, not who she would have liked to have been:

> I was taking cortisone which gives you a moon-face and my hair had fallen out to a large extent from the high fever, so I looked pretty much like the portrait," she wrote to a friend. "When I painted it I didn't look either at myself in the mirror or at the bird (a pheasant in the picture). I knew what we both looked like.

In her last years, she hobbled along on crutches, her bones made porous by the cortisone which kept her alive. Her face was often blotched with a rash that accompanies lupus and her body contorted from the arthritis and muscle pain that were her constant companions. Every menstrual period was an agonizing weeks-long bout with pain and severe bleeding; her blood vessels were inflamed and breaking down. But Flannery O'Connor wrote virtually until the day she died.

She hoped her work would endure, but she was sure that with her death, any interest in Flannery O'Connor personally would likewise be laid to rest:

> There won't be any biographies of me . . . for only one reason, lives spent between the house and the chicken yard do not make exciting copy.

Ah, Flannery, you could never have imagined that walking back and forth with you, stepping over the droppings of your beloved peacocks and peahens, hearing your soft Southern drawl, would be such a profound experience for so many people.

Companions Along the Way

Driskell, Leon V. & Brittain, Joan T., *The Eternal Crossroads: The Art of Flannery O'Connor,* Lexington, Univ. of Kentucky Press, 1971.

Eggenschwiler, David, *The Christian Humanism of Flannery O'Connor,* Detroit, Wayne State University Press, 1972.

Feeley, Kathleen, *Flannery O'Connor; Voice of the Peacock,* New Brunswick, Rutgers Univ. Press, 1972.

Fitzgerald, Sally, ed., *The Habit of Being: Letters of Flannery O'Connor,* New York, Farrar, Straus & Giroux, 1979.

Fitzgerald, Sally & Robert, eds., *Flannery O'Connor: Mystery and Manners,* New York, Farrar, Straus & Giroux, 1969.

Friedman, Melvin J. & Lawson, Lewis A., *The Added Dimension: The Art and Mind of Flannery O'Connor,* New York, Fordham Univ. Press, 2nd Edition, 1977.

Friedman, Melvin J. & Clark, Beverly Lyon, *Critical Essays on Flannery O'Connor,* Boston, G.K. Hall, 1985.

Montgomery, Marion, *Why Flannery O'Connor Stayed Home,* LaSalle, Sherwood Sugden, 1981.

O'Connor, Flannery, *The Complete Stories of Flannery O'Connor,* New York, Farrar, Straus & Giroux, 1971.

Stephens, Martha, *The Question of Flannery O'Connor,* Baton Rouge, Louisiana State Univ. Press, 1973.

Jalal Al-Din Rumi

The beat of a distant drummer is in your ears and no one else's. You hear a music no one else can hear. Such was the case with Jalal Al-Din Rumi; his friends and students greeted his outbursts and enthusiasm with skepticism. Had their master and teacher gone mad?

AS GENGHIS KHAN and his Mongol hordes swept across Asia, Baha'al-Din Valad gathered his family in the town of Balkh—which today lies within Afghanistan—and began his flight westward. He was an esteemed teacher, a mystical theologian, an observant Moslem and one of the pillars of a city rich in Islamic religious learning and fervor. All these traits, which elevated him in the eyes of his people, would work to his downfall if he were ever captured. He knew that when the Mongols conquered his city he would be among the first to be killed.

Companions Along the Way

Among his family members was his son, who he had named Jalal al-Din, "keeper of the faith." He was much like his father: well-educated in the Koran and the sayings of Mohammed, in philosophy and Persian literature, and so disciplined in religious practices that at the age of six he had voluntarily begun periodic fasting. The family embarked on a voyage that would last some 15 years until they would settle in a permanent new home. During that period the young boy would have a rich education, witnessing life in desert wastelands as well as in the great cities of Baghdad, Mecca and Damascus.

It was a time in Asian history when bloodbaths and political upheaval were commonplace and yet it was a time when religious and mystical activity were also at a peak. As is often the case, the worst of times and best of times coincided. Sufis like Baha'al-Din Valad looked beyond the calamities of the day; their pursuit of God could not be altered by the affairs of worldly powers. For the Sufis were in essence the monks of Islam; their goal was the direct realization of God and their path was through ascetic practices, meditation and prayer.

The family eventually settled in still another city rich in religious history and thought—Konya, a city to the south of Ankara in modern day Turkey. The city had been inhabited by Hittites, Persians and Romans. St. Paul and St. Barnabas had preached there. The Seljuks had captured it, then the Crusaders, only to lose the city back to the Seljuks. The reigning sultan of Konya was most eager to have Baha'al-Din Valad stay; he took the teacher to his roof and proudly pointed to the walls and towers he had erected to fortify his city. "Against torrents and the horsemen of the enemy you have put up a good defense," the Sufi said. "What protection do you have from the sighs and the moans of the oppressed which leap a thousand walls? Go and attempt to acquire the blessings of your subjects. This is the real stronghold."

The sultan was pleased with the forthrightness of Baha'al-Din Valad and he was appointed to a prestigious university position. Upon his death it was only natural that his son take his place. For Jalal al-Din—who would soon be called Rumi—was a scholar and an equally gifted teacher. He prayed five times a day, his face washed of any emotion, mouthing the solemn words of his faith. He prayed in private. Personally and professionally, he was ideal; his future seemed well mapped out for him.

In the year 1244, when Rumi was 37 years old, married, with children and by now a very respected, conventional mullah, a wandering mystic came to the city.

His name was Shams Tabriz and he wore an old, patched black wool cloak; he carried no possessions with him. Shams told of his many years of traveling, of visiting Sufi monasteries and the hermits living in the mountains. He was known as *parinda,* the "winged one," because he had wandered through so many lands in search of spiritual teachers. Shams' quest was simple —as the wandering holy men of every religion espouse— to somehow on earth find and partake of the hidden face of God to know God as directly as mortal man can.

The students of Rumi mocked Shams; he seemed still another of the foolish, mad wanderers they had seen before. They were more accustomed to a stable, disciplined, observant Muslim like their cherished Rumi. But on that cold November morning in 1244, as Rumi rode by the Inn of the Sugar Merchants in Konya, surrounded by his adoring students, he did not see the same man his students did. After a brief exchange, Shams fell to the ground before him, and Rumi dismounted and dropped to his knees before Shams. It was an apocalyptic moment in Islamic history. Each saw in the other a great and wise teacher and for the next three months the two were inseparable, living in a simple hut, barely taking time to eat or sleep as their discourses on the holy life made them oblivious to everything about them. Rumi would later write:

> Happy the moment when we are seated in the palace, thou and I.
> With two forms and with two figures but with one soul, thou and I.
> The colors of the grove and the voice of the birds bestow immortality.
> At the time when we came into the garden, thou and I.

The two men saw in each other the mirror of their own soul as well as the image of the Beloved One. And while the students grumbled at the loss of their teacher to this illiterate, unschooled pilgrim, Rumi and Shams talked on, intoxicated by the depth of divine love they had encountered. At first Shams instructed Rumi to remain silent and study Rumi's father's works and then abruptly told him to shut the books and never open them again. "There is study by reading and there is

Rumi

study by contemplating,'' Shams said. One day, when Rumi was lecturing to his students, Shams tore the book from Rumi's hands and threw it into the water. "You must live what you know,'' he chastised him.

This new awareness of God flooded Rumi's body. Here was a room filled with God and Shams had opened the door. This once sober, measured cleric could not contain his ecstasy and began mouthing spontaneous poems. He could see God everywhere and in everything. After passing by a goldsmith's shop and hearing the apprentices rhythmically pounding the sheets of gold, all he could hear was "Al-lah, Al-lah'' Rumi began whirling in the street to the hammers' beat, his hands extended, his head thrown back. From that simple encounter came a dance which would be at the core of the Mevlevi order of Sufis which Rumi founded, a whirling dance performed to the accompaniment of a baleful pipe and a drumbeat. This praise to God, which we today know as the dance of the whirling dervishes, was in essence a mobile meditation, where the mind could float free of the body and encounter the One to whom it was dedicated. Rumi couldn't understand the secret of his transformation; all he knew was that he was a changed man who could not go back to simply mouthing words and observing rituals. To Rumi, everything created was part of the eternal dance and he spontaneously expressed this union.

As Rumi's son would later write of his father:

Never for a moment did he cease from listening to music, and dancing;
Never did he rest by day or night.

Companions Along the Way

He had been a mufti: he became a poet;
He had been an ascetic: he became intoxicated by
Love.
'Twas not the wine of the grape: the illumined soul
drinks only the wine of Light.

Many of Rumi's students were hardly charmed by the
drastic change that had come over their teacher. Such a
dance, to musical accompaniment, was totally outside
Islamic tradition and practice. They forced Shams to
leave and when he returned, they soon put him to death.

But Rumi was now free himself—even with the death
of his beloved teacher—and over the next 40 years he
would write over 3,000 odes, some 35,000 couplets of
the most powerful mystical poetry Persia has ever witnessed. His *Mathnawi* is a rich collection of folklore,
proverbs and storytelling that has been called the greatest Muslim work since the Koran. His *Divan-i Shams*
translates in poetry the author's ecstatic religious experiences. The reader catches breathtaking glimpses of
the very madness of the Divine experience.

My hand always used to hold a Koran, but now it
holds love's flagon.
My mouth was filled with glorification, but now it
recites only poetry and songs . . .
Love came into the mosque and said, 'Oh great
teacher! Rend the shackles of existence! Why are
you tied to prayer carpets?'

To those who doubted him or speculated that he had
gone mad, he challenged them: "Your thoughts are the

Rumi

bar behind the door! Set the wood on fire! Silence,
heart!''

Whether he was scorned by those who thought he had
gone mad or praised by those who could see the reason
for his new-found bliss, Rumi went on. Never forgetting
the needs of the lower classes, who lived in virtual poverty, he wrote many of his poems with them in mind.
When the homeless came to his door, he sheltered them;
if a merchant was having a rough time, he made sure
that those followers from the higher strata of society
bought from him. His poems use everyday images that
all can understand:

> Thy truth is concealed in falsehood, like the taste
> of butter in buttermilk.
> Thy falsehood is this perishable body; thy truth is
> in the lordly spirit.
> During many years the buttermilk remains in view,
> while the butter has vanished as though it were
> naught,
> Till God sends a Messenger, a chosen Servant, to
> shake the buttermilk in the churn. . . .

And another poem:

> The parrot looking in the mirror sees
> Itself, but not its teacher hid behind,
> And learns the speech of man, the while it thinks
> A bird of its own sort is talking to it.
> So the disciple full of egoism
> Sees nothing in the Sheik except himself.
> The Universal Reason eloquent

Companions Along the Way

Behind the mirror of the Sheik's discourse—
The Spirit which is the mystery of man—
He cannot see. Words mimicked, learned by rote,
'Tis all. A parrot he, no bosom-friend.

Rumi was hardly conscious of the pearls of mysticism and practicality that he was uttering; it was only because some of his disciples followed him around and copied his spontaneous outbursts that we have such a wealth of material from him today.

Rumi talked about prayer in a way no one in Islam had done before. It was the language of the soul and needed no formula or great words or thoughts. It was the prayer of the simple shepherd, offering up to God "to sweep his little room, to comb his hair, to pick his lice, and to bring him a little bit of milk." Prayer could lead men and women to the realization that they need not kill their base qualities but should embrace them, integrating whatever they were and offering that up to God.

For those in the West who know little about Islam and its various sects, Rumi's life, thoughts and words are inspirational in themselves, indeed remarkably so, as he was preaching love while the Mongols conquered cities and slaughtered people at will. But the parallels in Christian mysticism are equally fascinating. Rumi saw that an ever-growing proximity to God annihilated the individual, until God lived in and through that person. "There is no room for two I's in the house," he said. This is surely the same sentiment as "Not I, but thou livest in me," a well-known biblical expression addressing the sublimation of self.

Rumi

Rumi based many of his poems and stories on the Koran. When he quotes Mohammed saying, "This world is the seedbed of the other world," he goes on to explain that each action in a person's life brings fruits for spiritual opportunity. He forshadows Thomas Merton, a Trappist monk who said something strikingly similar 700 years later in his *Seeds of Contemplation:*

> Every moment and every event of every man's life on earth plants something in his soul. For just as the wind carries thousands of winged seeds, so each moment brings with it germs of spiritual vitality that come to rest imperceptibly in the minds and wills of men.

The strict ascetism of the Sufis, their prayerfulness, fasting and concentrated pursuit of the mystical life, have many parallels in Western monasticism. It is interesting to note that as Rumi and his teachings were gaining popularity in the Islamic world, so too was Western monasticism burgeoning in Europe. Clearly, it was a time when the spiritual hunger of man and woman was producing great and inspirational figures in many faiths.

When he died in 1273, his funeral was a gathering of people that could not be limited by religious beliefs. He stood not only for Islam, but for a religion of universal love. Christians came, as did Jews and each, according to their own tradition and ritual, sent their long-time friend to the world he had been seeking. To this day, the stream of visitors to his tomb in Konya has not abated. Rumi spoke to the hearts and souls of men and women in search of God.

Companions Along the Way

After his death five Mevlevi monasteries, called *tekkes,* sprang up in Turkey as religious Sufis, with the Koran as their sustenance and Rumi as their guide, attempted to follow the narrow road to enlightenment. As the monasteries founded on the rule of St. Benedict would have a profound impact in the West, the Mevlevi monasteries exerted an enormous influence on Turkish culture, especially in music and poetry.

In 1925, the order was banished. Turkey was attempting to come into the modern age and these whirling dervishes did no useful work; they were considered foolish anachronisms in a country that badly wanted to shed its past. After the government padlocked the gates of the *tekkes,* townspeople came during the night and placed candles on the locks to express their sense of mourning.

Whirling dervishes seen today throughout the world are billed as "tourist attractions," but few people know their deep religious significance or know about the mystic-poet Rumi who brought the Mevlevi order into being. The flame that he enkindled is dim but not out, as religious boys and men—from those 12 years old to some in their 80s—continue in the dervish tradition. They carry on as their beloved Mevlana (our master) bid them to do in words he uttered not long before he died:

Do not search for me in the grave.
Look for me in the hearts of learned men.

Chittick, William C., *The Sufi Path of Love: The Spiritual Teachings of Rumi,* State University of New York Press, Albany, 1983.

Rumi

Friedlander, Ira, *The Whirling Dervishes: Being an Account of the Sufi Order Known as the Mevlevis and its Founder the Poet and Mystic Mevlana Jalalu'ddin Rumi,* Macmillan, New York, 1975.

Helminski, Edmund (trans.), *The Ruins of the Heart: Selected Lyric Poetry of al-Din Rumi,* Threshold Books, Putney, VT, 1981.

Nicholson, R.A., *Rumi: Poet and Mystic,* Mandala Books, London, 1978.

Schimmel, Annemarie, *The Triumphal Sun: A Study of the Works of Jalal al-Din Rumi,* East-West Publications, London, 1978.

IV. Pointing a Way

Ralph Waldo Emerson

Marcus Aurelius

Thomas Merton

Chief Seattle

Ralph Waldo Emerson

Sometimes, in looking at what is happening about us —in our world, our country, our community, our family or our job—it is obvious that change is occurring and a fresh approach is needed. Ralph Waldo Emerson, at a crucial time in American history, saw the needs of his country and boldly set out on a mission to change the hearts of his fellow citizens.

The America into which Ralph Waldo Emerson was born in 1803 was a raw, proud nation. Some 30 years before, the Declaration of Independence had rejected monarchy and set its course on a largely uncharted and perilous tack called democracy. No longer would men and women be ruled by those considered better by reason of birth or wealth. Instead, they would govern themselves.

Companions Along the Way

This new nation was free in large part due to the indomitable spirit that the Puritans embodied. They had come to what for them was a Promised Land, so that they might freely practice their faith. And they came with a resoluteness that not only kept and lived that faith, but tamed a wilderness and established order as settlements sprung up. They were as severe on themselves as the harsh land was, in turn, on them. The Puritans underscored man's basic depravity and the constant need for penance, and this concept produced the disciplined, hard-working midwife for the birth of a nation.

But as the young nation struggled through its infancy, and immigrants came from different countries, it was apparent that such Calvinistic rigidity could not last for long. What would replace it? Would the pride that Americans felt be forged into some kind of crude, nationalistic arrogance? Would the victor swagger on to demagogy? Now that political independence had been achieved, how would the citizens be prepared for its practice?

Emerson came from a family with a long history of Unitarian ministers. Unitarianism, with its emphasis on humanitarianism and the basic goodness of mankind as well as respect for scientific discovery, appealed to the reformists of the time, but in comparison to the rigid tenets of the Puritans it seemed tepid and weak, hardly the stuff from which to shape a country of upstanding citizens.

His father died while he was a boy and his mother was forced to take in boarders. Emerson lived in a kind of genteel poverty, but he was rich in the religious and ethical principles that his mother imbued and molded by the education provided by the best schools in the area: the Boston Latin and Harvard. After completing his education Emerson first tried teaching, but soon found it tedious and enervating and went back to Harvard for a divinity degree.

Emerson was an enormously successful young minister at Second Church, Boston. His sermons were little gems of theology and inspiration. And practicality. In "On Showing Piety at Home," Emerson sought to demonstrate to his parishioners the possibilities of holiness in their daily lives. He set high standards—purity for example—but was ultimately reasonable, allowing that "a single hour of perfect purity" was an awesome task. Meanwhile, as they sought perfection, he counseled his listeners at least to have a sense of humor and to be generous and affectionate.

However, after three years as a minister, Emerson found he could not go on reshaping his own religious beliefs—which centered around a trust in the spontaneous, intuitive faculties of man—to the pattern of his church's standards. He could not mouth prayers simply because they were called for at a certain point in a service; he could not administer the Lord's Supper simply because it was agreed upon day or time.

Something besides seeing to the needs of his parish was burning within him. Emerson wanted to take this unformed yet, he felt, basically decent American spirit, and shape a new generation of citizen. America's past was no template for its future. The representative form of government that democracy mandated needed citizens who were people of the highest virtue and Emerson clearly saw their formation as his life's mission.

Companions Along the Way

At 29 he resigned his appointment as a pastor, turned his back to history and his face toward uncertainty—and to the enormity of that task.

In a time before words could be transmitted electronically, the mass communication of the day was the public lecture, so Emerson took to the lecture circuit to propound his ideas. Although he wrote both prose and poetry, he was known predominantly as a speaker and soon he was enormously popular. One man, upon arriving late for a talk, declared it was better to miss an Emerson lecture than to attend one by anybody else.

Emerson characterized American men and women in the middle of the 19th century as people in chaos, crippled by a stultifying reverence for the past, unable to continue and complete the revolution that had set the country free. It was not a new dilemma; others in other lands had faced this before, but with "the same bankrupt look, to foregoing ages as to us, as of a failed world just re-collecting its old withered forces to begin again and try to do a little business."

Emerson called on Americans to boldly take another path:

We will walk with our own feet; we will work with our own hands; we will speak our own minds. The study of letters shall be no longer a name for pity, for doubt, and for sensual indulgence. The dread of man and the love of man shall be a wall of defense and a wreath of joy around all. A nation of men will for the first time exist, because each believes himself inspired by the Divine Soul which also inspires all men.

Ralph Waldo Emerson

Emerson combined a religious fervor and convincing rhetoric with a spirit of individualistic destiny that captured people's imagination. Like Socrates and Jesus in their day, Emerson was calling on people to be mistrustful of any society, even their own, that registered a claim of righteousness. History had proved that such "claims" inevitably transmuted into tyranny. Only through encouraging its citizenry to reach continually for the highest and most humane standards in themselves and their government could America be assured of not repeating the mistakes of the past. He held up Socrates as a man who "communicated to his disciples not hieroglyphical scripture to amuse the learned and awe the ignorant, but practical rules of life, adapted immediately to their condition and character, and little infected by the dogmas of their day."

Two of Emerson's best-known speeches laid out his approach clearly. "The American Scholar" in 1837 confronted the academic community with its smugness and short-sightedness and turned instead to every citizen for leadership and imagination; for each was a scholar, each had the ability to think and needed to take their responsibilities seriously. The following year, in his "Divinity School Address," he pronounced the churches of America—like the educators—tied to the past, stultified and dead in their learning, drowned by the torrent of words that flowed from the books they read. Later, he would spell out what was needed instead:

> . . . in society, besides farmers, sailors, and weavers, there must be a few persons of purer fire kept specially as gauges and meters of character;

167

persons of a fine detecting instinct, who note the
smallest accumulations of wit and feeling in the by-
stander . . . Perhaps too there might be room for the
exciters and monitors; collectors of the heavenly
spark with power to convey the electricity to others.

Emerson's impact was enormous, and his blend of religion and human potential found a ready audience,
especially in the young. He was not proposing a new system of thought or belief, but something as simple as a
disposition, an attitude by which to guide a life. There
was something admirable and appealing in this man who
was so obviously wrestling with as major an issue as how
to live a life in America. He admitted he, too, had a difficult time living by the standards he proposed and each
day had but a "few strong moments."

Unlike those who extolled the might and future of the
country, he would not give himself to the boom mentality. At once, he accepted his country for its principles
and soundly rejected its practice. In his lifetime, the
steam boat and railroad revolutionized travel and shipping, the telegraph linked cities and the trans-Atlantic
cable, continents. Mass production was introduced, the
westward expansion was beginning. While Emerson applauded such discoveries and expansion, he warned that
if man did not similarly develop, America, with the
Declaration of Independence as its inspiration, could
never transform itself and, by its example, remake the
world.

The disaffected and the reformers flocked to him,
espousing everything from woman's suffrage and the
abolition of slavery to pacifism and vegetarianism.

Ralph Waldo Emerson

Some were serious, some wild-eyed fanatics, but Emerson received them with grace and patience in his home in Concord, Massachusetts. He understood well their alienation and their hunger; he felt these himself. Many, after seeing him, felt their lives change. Still others, merely on reading a few pages of one of his books or a sentence in a magazine article by or about him, set themselves goals not unlike his. Slavery, economic injustice, poor education—his "disciples" attacked the major social ills of the time.

He was a beacon to them: the character of his power was the power of his character.

Emerson was an idealist, he was an American and he was a thinker who had, far beyond his contemporaries, taken a unique position. Theodore Parker, another imposing figure of the time, praised Emerson for his priorities, which he formulated as the "superiority of man to the accidents of man." He was, Parker wrote, "Eminently a child of Christianity and of the American idea," but "out of the church and out of the state." Emerson longed to give a description of the adventure of life and he proclaimed life an adventure open to everyone, not only the brilliant, bold or strong. Physical suffering, he said, could lead to heightened mental activity, helping people to discover themselves. The shy person, afraid to speak, might do much more to write his or her thoughts, rather than lose them in idle conversation.

While many praised him, Emerson also had vocal critics, who pronounced his thoughts vapid and cloudy, at best meditations during the callowness of youth, certainly not fit for grown men and women. With his advocacy of Transcendentalism, he was considered by some

169

to be nothing more than a heretic who had elevated intuition and individual responsibility to the status of religious tenets, to the exclusion of the standard creeds, ritual and safeguards built into mainline Catholic and Protestant Christianity as well as Judaism.

They were not entirely wrong. To Emerson, God was not only a deity outside, but one within each person. God was not praised by men and women going out to Him through worship services, Emerson said, but by allowing Him in. Emerson felt that the message of Christ had been bound securely between the covers of too many books and that preachers often proclaimed from "memory, not the soul." He wanted to infuse in the new American man and woman the same spirit that inspired the democratic movement which was alive in this country and spreading in Europe at the time. This would ideally be integrated into their religious beliefs, but if those beliefs called for unquestioning obeisance to ecclesiastical law or authority, Emerson held that the thinking person could not, in conscience, go along. "A foolish consistency is the hobgoblin of little minds," he said and "The perfect truth lay deeper than any actual expression of it."

Emerson did not claim to give readily digestible solutions; rather he saw himself as a questioning, seeking Everyman, endlessly learning, constantly turning over the occurrences of daily life.

Do not set the least value on what I do, or the least discredit on what I do not, as if it pretended to settle any thing as true or false. I unsettle all things.

Ralph Waldo Emerson

No facts are to me sacred; none are profane; I simply experiment, an endless seeker with no past at my back.

Asceticism or self-indulgence? A strict code of ethics, no morality at all? Such singular approaches were unacceptable to Emerson. To him, the perfect human was that man or woman who was perfectly free to do whatever he or she wished to do—but who in that freedom consistently chose what was right and in concordance with the will of God.

He was careful to point out that such freedom was not a license to trample over other people or their ideas. Such rugged individualists, vigilantes and exploiters were already all too well known in America, where "Manifest Destiny" was nearly a holy invocation. Responding to the critic who called his approach to life and advocacy of intuition an invitation to moral relativism and downright laziness, he said, "Let him keep its commandment one day."

While the Founding Fathers had struggled to make sure that religion would not prevail over secular affairs in America, Emerson felt that the only democracy that would be just and would last was a spiritual democracy. God's will would indeed be done on earth as it is in heaven if the Declaration of Independence and Bill of Rights, as well as the Bible guided a citizen's actions. The world might distract and others might disappoint, but Emerson's ideal man daily stood quietly but firmly for what was right and good.

The cry has gone up many times in America's history

that the country was nothing more than a materialistic, amoral society and that the voices of righteous men and women were needed to get us back on course. Who knows if today we are better or worse than previous generations? But one thing is sure: there is an emptiness that is felt, and it is of considerable magnitude. Emerson's is a voice from the past that can address our everyday concerns. As Matthew Arnold said, "He is the friend and aider of those who live in the spirit." And Lowell: "Emerson awakened us, saved us from the body of this death."

When Emerson died in 1882, a throng of his admirers and friends came to pay their respects on foot, by train, by horse and coach. Henry James called it the most touching funeral he had ever witnessed for a man of letters. For Emerson was more than a writer or speaker. He had found a way into people's souls, inspired them to live better lives and gave them the tools to do so.

Who knows what his true impact was. He lived at a crucial juncture in American history. Without him, might this nation have suffered an inner death? Might the racism and arrogance of his day so contaminated the body politic that it was invulnerable to the healing powers of justice and decency? Emerson pointed to another way, one that everyone could be involved in, to which everyone had a contribution to make. We live today still trying to complete the revolution started two hundred years ago, that the idealist soil from which this country sprang might bear a continuing rich harvest. Emerson echoes from the past, affirming and challenging with words that never grow old:

Ralph Waldo Emerson

A man is a golden opportunity. The line he must walk is a hair's breadth. The wise through excess of wisdom is made a fool.

Emerson, Ralph Waldo, *The Collected Works of Ralph Waldo Emerson,* Joseph Slater, *et al.* eds. 2 vols. Belknap Press, Cambridge, 1971.

Emerson, Ralph Waldo, *The Early Lectures of Ralph Waldo Emerson,* Stephen Whicher, *et al.* eds, 3 vols, Belknap Press, Cambridge, 1959-72.

McAleer, John, *Ralph Waldo Emerson: Days of Encounter,* Little, Brown, Boston, 1984.

Staebler, Warren, *Ralph Waldo Emerson,* Twayne, New York, 1973.

Wagenknecht, Edward, *Ralph Waldo Emerson: Portrait of a Balanced Soul,* Oxford University Press, New York, 1974.

Yannella, Donald, *Ralph Waldo Emerson,* Twayne, Boston, 1982.

Marcus
Aurelius

Marcus Aurelius certainly knew about having the upper hand in life, power over people. He was a man who could have done exactly as he pleased to whomever and with whomever he wished—and yet he didn't. He dramatically showed that it's not the system of belief that we profess, but how well we respond to our basic instincts for decency and justice, that ultimately matters.

ROMAN EMPERORS haven't come down through history with the best of reputations. As much as we know or care to remember about them, they seem to lump together as a rather arrogant bunch: some of them outright lunatics, others bloodthirsty and headstrong, none of them exactly what might be called prudent or considerate, hardly inspirational people for our life's journey. When you reigned by Divine Right, it seems, there was little cause to try to live like the rest of humanity. The people *had* their rules. You *were* the rule.

There is a glowing exception: Marcus Aurelius. The leader of the entire civilized world during his reign from 161 to 180 A.D., Marcus was also a shining example of justice, kindness, humility and, oddly enough—amazing good sense. No wonder Matthew Arnold called him "perhaps the most beautiful figure in history."

There was something special about the young Marcus, apparent even as a young boy. The Emperor Hadrian, known for both his masterful rule and for his cruelty, saw in Marcus' face and manner traits of extraordinary character. Unhappily married and childless, Hadrian felt sure that Marcus would mature into the kind of man into whose hands he could entrust the Empire, and spontaneously called him *Verissimus,* indeed a great honor for a child in Imperial Rome. *Verissimus* goes beyond even the formidable name Marcus had been given at birth: *Verus.* Truthful. Indeed, this was a young man with a reputation to live up to.

His parents had died when Marcus was still young and it was his grandfather who saw to his upbringing and education. There was no place for such a thing as formal religious training in Marcus' day, as the paganism practiced by the Romans involved little more than understanding what sacrifice pleased what god, on what day, presented in what fashion. The gods, it seemed, were more concerned with the art of the rites than the intent of the believer. Rome's "religion" was more a method of bargaining with these powerful deities than a set of standards by which to lead a life.

Well-to-do Romans like his grandfather, who found this kind of indoctrination rather anemic and who wanted to instill some sort of moral code in their children, sent them for instruction in one of two schools of Greek philosophy popular at the time. They were not that dissimilar: the Epicureans, whose ideal was a sort of peaceful detachment, a freedom from all disturbance; and the Stoics, who aspired to the harmony of all emotions. "Stoics" and "epicureans" stand for vastly different things today—practitioners of stubborn endurance and lavish living—but at the time each represented a genuine philosophy, with an elaborate system of beliefs to which at least lip service was paid. It is little different today if you think about it: scores of different religions and belief systems espouse high ideals, hordes of people profess to belong, but only a few come close to embodying those standards.

As his grandfather was a Stoic, young Marcus was destined to be trained in this school—and to be one of those rare people who not only heard the word but lived it.

The upper class in Rome lived extremely well and as morality was not really an issue, there was little to keep the wealthy from all forms of self indulgence and debauchery. But while other privileged young men went to the Roman Circus to drink and carouse with harlots, place their bets and cheer their favorite chariot drivers, Marcus lived strictly by the Stoic rule. He dressed in plain, short tunics, wore no jewelry, ate sparingly; his rooms were simply furnished. He hardened his body with outdoor sports, hunting and wrestling; he often slept on the ground in animal skins. Although he wasn't the most healthy or rugged boy, he showed enormous courage, stepping forward on the hunt to confront the fiercest boars. In triumph, he was never arrogant or proud; he shrugged off his accomplishments as well as his defeats. As for fawning over Hadrian and the key figures of the Roman court—good for any young man's career—Marcus would have none of it.

From his grandfather's words and example, Marcus learned early and well that gentleness and meekness were not the marks of the unmanly but of the truly indomitable and, conversely, that outbursts of anger and passion signaled weakness, not strength. It wasn't that Marcus was force-fed the Stoic line against his will. While the other boys mouthed all the right answers for their teachers and lived by another code, Marcus did not. It all made complete sense to him.

Pagans that they were, the Stoics held that only material things existed but they also believed that there was a spiritual force which acted through them. This force manifested itself not only in the various pagan deities, like Jupiter, Apollo, and Artemis, but in many other forms. There were the usual—fire, water, the wind—but the Stoics believed that this force was also present in reason, order and a just rule. This omnipotent force, this highest, ruling principle—*the* "god" of the Roman Stoics, as they understood it—willed and wanted all created matter and beings to work together for the common good. That "common good" could be and was interpreted in many ways to suit the needs of the day, but

Companions Along the Way

Marcus Aurelius believed in it in the purest sense. Only when the good of the whole was served was his god truly pleased, propitiated. And only when man worked in consort with the laws of nature and reason did man perform his highest function. Providence was in charge of the universe; virtue in his soul was the guiding principle for man. Virtue, plain and simple, was what the Stoics were about and it was to this end that Marcus dedicated his life.

And, of course, his friends laughed. Why make it so hard for yourself, Marcus? they chided. Try as he might, Marcus couldn't convince them that he wasn't living as he did just to suffer. Far from it. Virtue *was* happiness.

When his day finally came and the Roman Senate was ready to elect Marcus Aurelius emperor, there was a single, strong dissenting vote—Marcus himself. He stood before the senators and confessed he had not sought and did not want the power and the responsibility of the purple mantle. He was sure he was not worthy of their trust.

Perhaps they wondered too, as the celebrations began, whether this upstanding man would change once the crown was upon his head. They had seen it happen so many times when men came to power in Rome; earnest promises withered in the daily press of overseeing such a vast empire; principles were recast juggling so many conflicting viewpoints and conniving aspirants.

Marcus came to office well trained, disciplined, with the best of intentions to be "unspotted by pleasure, undaunted by pain," but when we look at other circumstances of his life, it's apparent that they were far from

178

Marcus Aurelius

being conducive to his living as a just, moral man. He was tested again and again by events, people and fate. His wife was openly unfaithful, enamored with too many a gladiator, most of his children died young and, just as he became emperor, it seemed every rebel warlord and barbarian chieftain who could muster up an army did so. In the early years of his reign, the Tiber River overflowed its banks and floods destroyed entire sections of the city as well as huge amounts of grain, causing widespread famine. A plague brought back by his legions further ravaged the Roman citizenry, killing thousands.

Not only was his wife Faustina a worthless wench but she also plotted with Avidius Cassius in an attempt to overthrow him. They must have thought that Marcus would be a pushover, and anyhow just too nice a fellow to be on the throne. But when the revolution failed and Cassius' head was brought to Marcus Aurelius, he refused this gift of vengeance. Can you imagine the look on the faces of those faithful followers carrying in Cassius' head—sure they would be richly rewarded—when they were told the Emperor wasn't interested in their trophy?

And instead they might have been lectured: "Whatsoever any man either does or says, thou must be good. Does any man offend? It is against himself that he does offend: why should it trouble you?"

His was an exemplary life, but Marcus was hardly perfect in his pursuits. Like most of us, he had his blind spots. One was a new group that was gaining some popularity during his reign. They were called Christians. Seemingly, they should have been to his liking, standing for many of the Stoic principles, but the Christians were just too passionate for Marcus' taste. They didn't treasure reasoning as he did; as far as he could see, it had little place in their religion. And, unlike the other sects that proliferated at the time, and were for the most part tolerated, these Christians would not fall in line and honor the Roman gods—as the other groups did, so that they could go on with their practices.

Although he made slaves' lives easier, the courts fairer and insured that poor and fatherless children would be cared for, history reveals he did nothing to see that Christians were not persecuted and many were brutally martyred.

We know best of Marcus Aurelius' character not from his exploits on the battlefield—although he was a successful commander-in-chief—nor from some authorized biography (the usual way for figures of the time to have the most favorable version of their story told) but rather from his *Meditations*. These remarkable reflections were started, oddly enough, when he was at war with the Quadi at Granua, in what would now be Yugoslavia. At a time when most men would be pounding their chests and thundering for victory, Marcus quietly jotted by candlelight in the solitude of his tent. History has quite correctly enshrined him as "the most peaceful of warriors."

Many scholars have agreed that except for the New Testament, the *Meditations* are unique in the ancient world for their inwardness, self-scrutiny, demand for high standards, indeed for their "religious" feeling.

In the *Meditations* Marcus Aurelius, continuing the

180

Marcus Aurelius

self-examination that involved him throughout his life, performs an exacting self-appraisal to discern what will bring a man happiness. This is no intellectual exercise or the outpouring of a heart yearning to be good or right. Not at all. Marcus simply talks to himself—hardly expecting that his musings will survive him—about how he needs to act and think to be a satisfied man. And this is what he concludes:

> If thou shalt find anything in this mortal life better than righteousness, than truth, temperance, fortitude . . . apply thyself unto it with thy whole heart, and that which is best wheresoever thou dost find it, enjoy freely.

To his credit, Marcus is never self-consciously unctuous or really confessional in his *Meditations*. His openness and sincerity come through resoundingly. It's hard to realize that this was a man who ruled most of the known world at the time. He sounds more like a simple monk away in his hermitage. Just to sit with the *Meditations* in the twentieth century is to feel a cool breeze blowing from the second.

> Let death surprise me when it will, and where it will, I may be a happy man, nevertheless. For he is a happy man who in his lifetime dealeth unto himself a happy lot and portion. A happy lot and portion is: good inclinations of the soul, good desires, good actions.

Marcus saw clearly that each individual's job was to overcome himself or herself, not to give in to our most base desires (no matter how wonderful they may feel for the moment), and strive every day to be stronger than the day before. He knew that this could not be willed at a moment's notice or marshalled up when under pressure or in danger, so he advocated drilling the soul in right principles on a daily basis. He knew well that he couldn't expect to control his temper at a crucial moment if he had never done it before. He saw living as more a wrestler's art than a dancer's; it was essential "To teach a man whatsoever falls upon him, that he may be ready for it and not thrown down."

He venerated reason and nature, and Marcus Aurelius felt that if he did not violate the laws of either, he had nothing to fear. And, he never trembled over what *might* occur; he never wasted time going over scenarios of potential disasters. As his reason had served him in the past, it would not fail him in the future. Of course, he knew that an enemy could defeat or overthrow him using unethical means, but Marcus Aurelius rested in the surety that he, himself—as a person—could never be compromised.

> Let them behold and see a man, that is a man indeed, living according to the true nature of man. If they cannot bear with me, let them kill me. For better were it to die, than so to live as they would have me.

In our day when "going for it" and "you can have it all" are the battle cries, when the word "profitable" often means a bottom line accounting of whether money was made or lost, it's interesting to see how Marcus considered this icon term of an often materialistic world.

182

Marcus Aurelius

If they mean profitable to man as he is a rational man, stand thou to it, and maintain it; but if they mean profitable, as he is a creature, only reject it. . . . Never esteem of anything as profitable, which shall ever constrain thee either to break thy faith, or to lose thy modesty; to hate any man, to suspect, to curse, to dissemble, to lust after anything that requireth the secret of walls or veils.

He advocated being gentle to those in error, forgiving of enemies and flatly stated that there was only one impiety, namely, injustice. It would be wonderful to hear some of Marcus Aurelius' pronouncements on our world today, ruled as it is by people who advocate justice only when it conforms to their particular religious, political or economic system. Marcus Aurelius said over and over that all men are made for each other. "Either then teach them better, or bear with them." He knew that ultimately only good would ever overcome evil. And besides, "The best kind of revenge is not to become like unto them."

Just as remarkable was the man's flexibility; again not a trait that many Emperors—or even some modern day bosses—practice. Marcus Aurelius, proclaimed a divine ruler, knew he didn't have all the answers and he put great accent on valuing other people's opinions rather than merely trusting his own. In fact, he actually advocated being ready to change your mind. To do so was actually to learn, he exhorted. Marcus was ready to allow change in anything, everything: if anyone found a system of beliefs better than that which he espoused, that person had the obligation to accept and live by it.

Companions Along the Way

Although he inadvertently—though quite clearly—echoed the Judeo-Christian ethos of loving God and every man and woman as you do yourself, and prefigured contemporary contemplative spirituality with his intense and continuing self-examination, Marcus Aurelius was neither a man of faith nor of hope. He would have been insulted to be labeled with such foolishness, to be toting such superfluous, unnecessary baggage on this journey called life. He didn't need to pray or try in any way to commune with or reach out to that higher power he knew was present in the universe. As a true Stoic, he carried his "god" within him. To Marcus, the Christians must have appeared to be at a severe disadvantage—answering to a Power outside them.

As ardent a Stoic and pagan as he was, though, it's fascinating to find hints within the *Meditations* that Marcus wanted more. It was somehow unsatisfying to him to think that at the end of his life he would merely be absorbed into the cosmos.

> How then stands the case? Thou hast taken ship, thou hast sailed, thou art come to land, go out, if to another life, there also shalt thou find gods, who are everywhere.

Life was much simpler for our Companion Marcus Aurelius, because he understood the rules—simpler, perhaps, but harder as well. But he always knew where he stood. He didn't have to ask anyone "How am I doing?"; he only asked himself. He saw himself not with a crown or a general's mantle, hardly as immortal, but only as a simple, naked man with limited ability and but a fraction of time on this earth.

184

Marcus Aurelius

Near the end of his *Meditations,* after tussling with the host of problems every human being faces, he finally asks himself the ultimate question: "What is thy profession?"

He wastes no time with any fancy preludes. "To be good," he unequivocally states. Legions of saints and holy men and women have professed little more.

Marcus Aurelius goes down in history not as a seminal or original thinker, not as a great philosopher or leader, but as a man who quite simply lived what he believed. He was tempted to seek revenge, was impatient with stupidity or faithlessness, and was lured by ambition and wealth, but he refused to give in to venality. Frederick the Great cast a discerning eye back in time and pronounced: "Marcus Aurelius, of all human beings, carried virtue to its highest point."

Aurelius, Marcus, *Meditations,* New York, Heritage Press, 1956.

Farquharson, Arthur, *Marcus Aurelius: His Life and His World,* New York, William Salloch, 1951.

Sedgwick, Henry, *Marcus Aurelius: A Biography,* New York, AMS Press, 1971.

Thomas Merton

Let Thomas Merton's words introduce him:
...if you want to identify me, / ask me not where I live, / or what I eat, / or how I comb my hair, / but ask me what I am living for, / in detail, / and ask me what I think / is keeping me from living fully / for the thing I want to live for.
— My Argument With the Gestapo

THAT CONFUSED and frightened week of December, 1941, America entered World War II. All across the country young men were volunteering to serve and protect their country, vowing vengeance for the attack on Pearl Harbor and swift retribution to the Nazis in Europe. But on December 10, a rather plain-faced, sandy-haired man of 27 appeared not at a recruiter's office, but instead at an undistinguished set of buildings

186

Thomas Merton

tucked into the rolling Kentucky hills near Bardstown. He knocked at the high wooden gate and asked admittance to the Trappist monastery of Our Lady of Gethsemani. This was to be no enlistment. It was far more serious. There would be no release. No vacations. Few visitors, censored mail. Medieval living conditions. Men who came to the Trappists knew that they were choosing the most rigorous order within the Catholic Church; the only "success" in this commitment was to spend the rest of their lives in silence within those cloistered walls.

The world about him might have regarded Thomas Merton as sadly out of step, escaping from the real and present dangers of the most horrible war in our history. But Merton had another task to accomplish. In becoming the "marginal man" he labeled himself as a monk, Merton knew he was going right to the heart of man's needs. He was convinced that to be at a place where prayer was at the core of life was to be in the midst of a suffering world. In a certain way, he was no different from his friends joining the armed services. But he was offering his life not only for his country; Merton was giving it to the entire world.

For every vital, quixotic person like Merton who makes—and keeps—such a lifelong commitment, there is usually a sequence of events, and often a single moment, that bring about their decision. Merton eloquently told about his conversion in his best-selling autobiography, *The Seven Storey Mountain,* but what truly motivated him to join the Trappists was that as a college student, for the first time in his life, he had experienced forgiveness for the excesses of his early life —and he felt loved, not in spite of what he had done, but

187

simply because he was a creation of God. He had encountered "mercy within mercy within mercy," as he later described his concept of God. He was released and he wanted to repay that debt; life finally had meaning and he wanted his days on this earth to reflect his thanks. And he had found a companion for his life's journey, a voice he could trust, one he wanted to direct him.

Merton had been a modern day St. Augustine in his youth, spent both in Europe and America; a brilliant, multilingual student, eagerly pursuing whatever taste his appetite hungered for at the moment: art, music, architecture, history—carousing, drink, women. He had even fathered an illegitimate child while a student at Cambridge University.

He lived more by impetus than intention, giving into whatever he thought would please him for the moment. Indeed, many of those moments were succulent and delightful; the hedonistic life is certainly not without its benefits! But the inevitable interludes, the quiet times away from the crowd's laughter, pounded at his brain. As Merton wrote in *The Seven Storey Mountain:*

> [I had] walked out into the world that I thought I was going to ransack and rob of all its pleasures and satisfactions. I had done what I intended, and now I found that it was I who was emptied and robbed and gutted. What a strange thing! In filling myself, I had emptied myself. In grasping things, I had lost everything. In devouring pleasures and joys, I had found distress and anguish and fear.

While at Columbia University, as his friend Robert Lax describes, "books just started falling into his hands." A volume in a Fifth Avenue bookstore window on medieval philosophy by Etienne Gilson somehow caught his eye. He read another work by the mystical artist and poet William Blake. Other books by authors in whom he formerly had no interest—Gerard Manley Hopkins, St. Bernard and Evelyn Waugh—he devoured. He stayed up all night to read *Ends and Means* by Aldous Huxley. A strange, foreign notion slowly but definitely came clear to him: a life without the normal comforts of society, without giving in to every whim he might have, had enormous possibilities. Asceticism was not merely denial, but an age-old pathway to one's God —and one's true self. A purposeful detachment wasn't a "weird and ugly perversion of nature" as Merton had long believed, but a way of opening up to God and the heights of worldly joy. It offered a way to come closer to that "mercy within mercy within mercy."

The urge to live for something beside himself was there, but so was the old Merton:

> I began to desire to dedicate my life to God, to His service. The notion was still vague and obscure, and it was ludicrously impractical in the sense that I was already dreaming of mystical union when I did not even keep the simplest rudiments of the moral law. . . . I remember how learnedly and enthusiastically I could talk for hours about mysticism and the experimental knowledge of God, and all the while I was stoking the fires of the argument with Scotch and soda.

When Thomas Merton decided to join the Trappists, he did it not to suffer or to atone for his sins. He entered with a spirit of happiness. He had found a sensible way to live a life. An orphan since the age of 15, he had also found a home. Other men and women move from place to place, job to job, friend to friend, but Merton knew that for him true freedom meant confinement, less stimuli rather than more, routine rather than diversion.

When Merton was accepted at Gethsemani, he made a firm promise to leave his secular self outside the gate —and never to write again. He wanted to live and die unnoticed by the world, rising at 2 a.m., sleeping on a straw mattress, drinking weak barley coffee, fasting, spending long hours in prayer, praising and thanking his God.

His abbot had other ideas for Thomas Merton. He knew he had an extraordinary young man whose talents should not be wasted. Merton at first resisted the abbot's request that he write his life's story. He had made a decision he believed to be absolutely necessary for his survival. After all, it was clearly what God wanted for him! It frightened him to drag that egotistical, self-involved part of himself into the monastery. How could he encounter God if he again became so wrapped up in himself?

His superior insisted and Merton finally acquiesced. He had no great hopes for the book—if it would ever be published—but he began to write. He was not at all sure he was doing the right thing, but this man who left the world and a promising literary career, who was content to be a simple, anonymous monk in an out-of-the-way monastery, eventually became the source for conversion and transformation for thousands—and the inspiration to simply go on for untold millions. His sixty books, together with the torrent of letters, articles, essays, reviews and poems that came from behind the Gethsemani walls, put Thomas Merton more in the midst of humanity than ever would have been possible had he lived in the world.

After *The Seven Storey Mountain* was published, Merton was well known across America, but he did nothing to bolster his image, never traded on his fame or asked for special treatment at the monastery. He rarely left the cloister, granted no interviews—but, still being the outgoing Merton, had scores of correspondents and friends—and for 27 years lived little different from the rest of the Gethsemani monks. Many of them to this day marvel at how—or when—he was able to produce his great body of work. Like them, he spent long hours in communal and private prayer and performed his share of the manual labor—doing it all in typical Merton style, with great gusto.

His early books dealt with his conversion, the Trappist life, his discovery of God and the necessity for everyone to take time in contemplation so that they might rise above daily events and listen to the yearnings of their deepest selves. The books were enormously successful and Merton could have gone through life dealing with those subjects—keeping Trappist superiors, the Church hierarchy and his many readers quite happy. But he couldn't. Feeling the seismic shocks of the late 1950s and early 1960s, Merton knew drastic changes were imminent, that the upheaval over race and war and social justice would revolutionize the world's thinking. He was one of those people who could clearly see events before they occurred—he forecast the race riots of the 1960s in sadly precise detail.

As he had once found it so necessary to turn his back on the world, he now knew he had to re-enter it in his own way. It had never been done before: a cloistered monk addressing the most pressing issues of the day, current events, happenings that he could not see. Merton read, and prayed, and listened to his Companion—and he began to write.

He was a source of inspiration to people involved in civil rights, disarmament and those opposed to the war in Vietnam—but this time, an embarrassment to his Trappist superiors. The impact of this "marginal man," supposedly in his cell, in silence, his thoughts only on the hereafter, was felt from picket lines to the Pentagon, from church pulpits to the Vatican. Finally, Rome said enough: as a monk, he could write about mysticism and contemplation, but he was not to publish anything about the atrocities of war, the inequalities of racial bias, the burgeoning nuclear arsenal.

Of course, Merton was dismayed and furious. Those were the crucial issues of the day; the very things people needed to consider to not only save their souls, but their lives. But, convinced though he was, he was also a man wise enough to know that just to be right was not enough, that continual disobedience would only harden the very people—the generals as well as his Trappist superiors—he wanted to change. As he wrote to a friend, "It would reassure them in every possible way that they are incontrovertibly right and make it even more impossible for them ever to see any kind of new light on the subject.''

Although he would not be openly defiant toward the Church and the superiors to whom he had vowed his obedience, Merton was not about to let anyone completely blunt what his conscience had told him he must do. He could have spent years fighting the censors, but at one point, Merton finally gave in to them, knowing in his heart that if what he had to say had legitimacy and held some grain of truth, it would win out in the end. A prudential judgment by a man who knew little moderation, but enormous discipline.

Merton acquiesced; he promised not to *publish* anything on those controversial issues; promised, it must be added, with a typical Merton wink. Instead of sending his controversial thoughts on everything from the Vietnam War to the Church's unbending stand on birth control to a publisher, he sent letters and essays to his friends. Those friends disseminated Merton's material further. A good number eventually found their way to magazine and newspaper offices. Merton's views were heard, and years after his Church had censored him, the monk's far-seeing writings eventually came to form the basis of official Church documents.

Perhaps Merton's writings were so popular when they first appeared (and still enjoy popularity) today because every reader seems to feel Merton is talking to each of them personally. Without ever being sanctimonious or preachy, he showed people how to be *fully* religious without the necessity of being *formally* religious. He virtually invented a new way of writing about God and the groaning of each person's soul. He knew from his own experience the hunger within man and the counter-vailing pressures of everyday life in the world. He pointed toward a way simple and sure, and available to every seeker.

Solitude is not found so much by looking outside the boundaries of your own dwelling as much as by staying within. Solitude is a deepening of the present, and unless you look for it in the present, you will never find it.

He was a painfully honest man for whom writing was a form of confession, putting words on paper a necessary step to squarely facing himself.

We are at liberty to be real or to be unreal. We may be true or false. The choice is ours. We may wear now one mask and now another, and never, if we so desire, appear with our own true face. But we cannot make these choices with impunity. Causes have effects. And if we lie to ourselves, and to others, then we cannot expect to find truth and reality whenever we happen to want them.

But exacting as he might be on himself and his readers in the pages of his books, Merton was not so with any-one personally. When he saw a face or read a letter, somehow that soul opened up to him. Visitors to the monastery, to the hermitage where he lived the last three years of his life, the thousands of people with whom he corresponded, found him warm and humorous, never judgmental, surely never condemnatory. He preached no dogma, never asked a person to convert to his Church or his way of thinking. Merton never forgot that he too had felt the pain of utter confusion and seemingly unforgivable sin and he was not about to heap hot coals upon anyone else's head. Just keep going, Merton would say, God is with you. He loves you, regardless. Don't expect results, he would advise those fatigued with trying to right some of the world's wrongs; that's not important. Your effort, your nature, the way you embrace your enemy even as you confront him—those are the ways to win hearts and minds. As Flannery O'Connor possessed a "habit of being"—a completely natural, comfortable, reassuring way of dealing with people—so did Merton.

He was an ebullient man, given to great excesses and mood swings, but he was, above all, a man of faith in God, a man who was a positive thinker before that term took on its tinny, commercial, facile connotations. Each day, he firmly believed, had its magic, pregnant opportunities; as he wrote in *New Seeds of Contemplation:*

> Every moment and every event of every man's life on earth plants something in his soul. For just as the wind carries thousands of winged seeds, so each moment brings with it germs of spiritual vitality that come to rest imperceptibly in the minds and wills of men. Most of these unnumbered seeds perish and are lost because men are not prepared to receive them. For such seeds as these cannot spring up anywhere, except in the good soil of freedom, spontaneity and love.

Merton continued to be a fertile ground for those winged seeds, right up to the end of his life. He became deeply interested in Eastern religions—much to the scandal of many within the Church, who traditionally dismissed these beliefs and practices as pagan and foolish—seeing in them a depth of spirituality often sorely lacking in his own faith. That Buddhism, Sufism, Taoism, mandalas and koans were outside the accepted Christian path to holiness meant nothing to him. They provided other ways, just as valid.

Another winged seed came in a strange form to him. Over 50 years old, having spent a quarter century in a monastery, Thomas Merton fell deeply in love with a young nurse about 20 years old whom he met while in a hospital to have surgery on his neck. He had never run from emotion, inspiration or conflict before—be they of the world, sent by God or in the irresolute area between—and he did not run from her. He kissed her lips, smelled the sweetness of her perfume, wrote her soaring, romantic poems and meanwhile prayed to God not to look away during this intoxicating and terrifying time of his life.

What was he to do? Leave the Trappists behind and marry her? What was God saying to him? What did he want of himself?

It was the most difficult decision he ever had to make and finally Thomas Merton saw where his place was. He reaffirmed his commitment to the Trappists. As wonderful as life would be with "M.," the monastic life was where he belonged. He yearned for her, but held by his choice.

A year later, attending a conference in Bangkok, Thailand, on his first extended trip outside the monastery in 27 years, he was accidentally electrocuted. Had

Thomas Merton

he not died such an untimely death, where would he be today? Surely no place safe, secure or predictable. This unflagging searcher, clear-eyed and open, remains a tireless Companion whose footsteps still echo around this globe.

Forest, James, *Thomas Merton: A Pictorial Biography,* Paulist Press, Mahwah, NJ, 1980.

Furlong, Monica, *Merton: A Biography,* Bantam Books, New York, 1981.

Merton, Thomas, *The Asian Journal of Thomas Merton,* Naomi Burton Stone *et al* eds. New Directions, New York, 1973.

_____, *The Monastic Journey,* ed. by Patrick Hart, Doubleday, New York, 1978.

_____, *New Seeds of Contemplation,* New Directions, New York, 1972.

_____, *The Seven Storey Mountain,* Harcourt, Brace, New York, 1948.

_____, *Wisdom of the Desert,* New Directions, New York, 1970.

Padavano, Anthony, *The Human Journey: Thomas Merton, Symbol of the Century,* Doubleday, New York, 1982.

Chief
Seattle

When our lives are humming along and progress seems inevitable, it's not difficult to exhibit confidence and grace. But what happens when events conspire to lessen our chances and our influence? Chief Seattle lived at such a time in the history of Native Americans, and proved himself a great statesman in a time of tremendous change.

THE SHOUT went up in the village along Puget Sound and the Suquamish tribespeople rushed to the shoreline to get a better look at the incredible scene. Among the throng was a six-year-old boy known as Sealt, the son of a female slave his father had captured in a raid.

Chief Seattle

The year was 1792. The Suquamish marveled at what they were seeing: was it a whale, with a tree growing out of its back? Or perhaps a great bird of the sea with enormous white wings? An island gone adrift? A dream? Such apparitions had been reported to the North, but the Suquamish had never seen such an object in the waters off their coast.

Beyond the sighting of this strange floating object, these were confusing times for the Native American tribes in an area that would later become known as Washington State. Strange men with no color at all to their skin were beginning to come to the land which had once been theirs alone. A disease the tribes had never experienced before had proved to be mightier than any warrior they had ever encountered. Entire communities had been decimated, their old and young alike unable to stand up to this ruthless foe called smallpox.

Life had never been easy for the Native American tribes in the Pacific Northwest; the stronger were constantly raiding the weaker, killing the men and taking women and children as slaves. But the land itself was beautiful and bountiful, rich with berries and wild onions; elk and deer were plentiful; bear and beaver provided skins and the ocean yielded a rich bounty of salmon and shellfish. But now, with the arrival of a man called Vancouver and his ship *Discovery,* the Suquamish would find their lives changed still more.

As the white man was making his first small settlements amidst the Suquamish, the young boy Sealt was growing into manhood. While he was impressed with the cloth and warm blankets the white man traded, the objects of metal and the fine guns he possessed, Sealt was by necessity more taken up with the daily life of his people. Because of his undistinguished lineage, he was considered of low birth, hardly on a par with the other boys of the village, but as Sealt grew up to be a tall, husky brave, it became apparent he was destined for a key role in his tribe. What he was not granted by birth he had by instinct and he quickly developed into an excellent marksman and hunter. While he had a reputation for bravery, he also was prized for his ingenuity.

He was no more than 20 years old when word came that a huge raiding party was preparing to attack his village. The elders didn't know how to defend the tribe against the superior numbers of the raiders, but Sealt developed the strategy that saved his people from sure destruction. At a bend in the Green River, he directed that a tree be felled so that it lay across the channel. The attack came, as expected, at night, but when the intruders rounded the bend on the fast moving river, they ran into the trap. Their canoes upended, they were no match for Sealt's warriors.

After this stunning victory over an enemy which had his people badly outnumbered, Sealt was chosen chief, not only of his tribe, but of others in the vicinity. He was later described by a settler as a man ". . . with a Roman countenance and black curly hair, the handsomest Indian I have ever seen."

He would eventually be called Chief Seattle. Ruling his people for the next half century, Seattle would prove over and over again to be more than a fierce warrior. He could see that the brave boasts of the young might bring cheers and admiration, but were as pale as the white man's face when it came to battle: the spear and arrow were no match for musket and cannon. Seattle saw that diplomacy, not belligerence, was needed and he developed into a wise and just leader, one true to his own heritage and sensitively aware of the role a chief in Washington, D.C. would play in the lives of Native Americans.

He recognized that the numbers of his people were declining, while those of the white man grew and he saw that in so many ways, the white man could do things the tribespeople could not. But Seattle could never quite understand their ways.

> To us the ashes of our ancestors are sacred and their resting place is hallowed ground. You wander far from the graves of your ancestors and seemingly without regret. Your religion was written upon tablets of stone by the iron finger of your God so that you could not forget. The Red Man could never comprehend nor remember it. Our religion is the tradition of our ancestors—the dreams of our old men, given them in the solemn hours of night by the Great Spirit; and the visions of our sachems, and is written in the hearts of our people.

Just as keenly as Seattle knew the ways of the forests in which he had hunted since he was a boy, he was instinctively aware of the changing times in which he lived. He wanted a better life for his people and whatever was required in that quest he was willing to do. He and many of the native people of Puget Sound converted to Christianity, yet while Seattle lived the tenets of the new faith, he never abandoned the precious beliefs of his ancestors. He instituted morning and evening prayer, because he thought it wise to give honor to God; he prohibited the practice of revenge murder so the cycle of killing could stop. And when the chief named Lincoln declared the slaves free, Seattle released his own.

He believed in the dignity of his people—and he inferred that dignity upon these strangers who had come to his land as well, though they often proved underserving. His wisdom was profound; he was truly the epitome of the philosopher-king yet he had no formal education; it is a pity we know so little about him.

What we do know of Seattle is pieced together from the accounts of the traders and settlers of the time. The eloquent words attributed to him may not be exactly as he spoke them, written down as they were years later but the essence of Seattle, and his native dignity, is surely there. His words haunt us today as we look back on the abuses heaped upon Native Americans, the treaties broken, the promises unkept.

> Yonder sky that has wept tears of compassion upon my people for centuries untold, and which to us appears changeless and eternal, may change. Today is fair. Tomorrow it may be overcast with clouds. My words are like the stars that never change. Whatever Seattle says the great chief at Washington can rely upon with as much certainty as he can upon the return of the sun or the seasons.

Seattle, once so hopeful that his people and the settlers could mutually adapt and live in peace, saw the situation worsen as he grew older. He agreed to sell the lands his people had always roamed so that the city that now bears his name should grow and prosper. The payments were held back and even when they came he saw his people degenerate before his eyes. The white man's powerful spirits made them into drunks, their reservation was a breeding ground for poverty and disease. And yet he stood before his own people with honor and turned his steady gaze and his words to those in whom he had placed his trust. He was awed by what the white man could do, but he was keenly aware of his shortcomings.

A few more moons. A few more winters. And not one of the descendants of the mighty hosts that once moved over this broad land or lived in happy homes, protected by the Great Spirit, will remain to mourn over the graves of a people—once more powerful and hopeful than yours. But why should I mourn at the untimely fate of my people? Tribe follows tribe, and nation follows nation, like the waves of the sea. It is the order of nature, and regret is useless. Your time of decay may be distant, but it will surely come, for even the White Man whose God walked and talked with him as friend with friend, cannot be exempt from the common destiny. We may be brothers after all. We will see.

Let him be just and deal kindly with my people, for the dead are not powerless. Dead, did I say? There is no death, only a change of worlds.

Within the scant amount of lore that we have about Seattle, perhaps there is no more touching—and disturbingly contemporary—a passage than that contained in a letter he was reputed to have sent to President Franklin Pierce in 1854. Was it read in Washington? Will it be taken to heart today?

We know that the White Man does not understand our ways. One portion of the land is the same to him as the next, for he is a stranger who comes in the night and takes from the land whatever he needs. The earth is not his brother, but his enemy, and when he has conquered it, he moves on. He leaves his fathers' graves, and his children's birthright is forgotten. The sight of your cities pains the eyes of the Red Man. But perhaps it is because the Red Man is a savage and does not understand.

There is no quiet place in the white man's cities. No place to hear the leaves of spring or the rustle of insect's wings. . . . The Indian prefers the soft sound of the wind darting over the face of the pond, the smell of the wind itself cleansed by a mid-day rain or scented with a pinion pine. The air is precious to the Red Man. For all things share the same breath—the beasts, the trees, the man. Like a man dying for many days, he is numb to the stench. . . . All things are connected. Whatever befalls the earth befalls the sons of the earth.

The whites, too, shall pass—perhaps sooner than the other tribes. Continue to contaminate your bed, and you will one night suffocate in your own waste . . . We might understand if we knew what it was that the White Man dreams, what he describes to his children on the long winter nights, what visions he burns into the minds, so they will wish for tomor-

row. But we are savages. The White Man's dreams
are hidden from us.

To some of the settlers of the city we now call Seattle,
Chief Seattle was perhaps a rather laughable old man. He
would appear in town clad in an old pair of pants, a shirt
and Hudson's Bay blanket—and on special occasions, in
a top hat and worn frock. The treaties he had told his
people would insure their future were worth nothing and
yet he came, time and again, to defend whatever rights he
could. He remained a protector to his people and he was
sought as a judge in tribal councils, but those among the
most enterprising of the white men could smile and know
they had bested one who once had been so mighty.

As he neared death, he distributed the few belongings
he had—old clothes, tin cans, some fishhooks, a mule-
shoe, a horseshoe—and he made a simple request. "I
have only one thing to ask and that is for my good
friend—always my friend—to come to my funeral and
shake hands with me before I am laid in the ground."
Those gathered around his bed could not figure who this
'friend' was; but as his funeral demonstrated it was not
one person, but hundreds.

It was a strange event, for the white man rarely acknowledged the death of a Native American, much less
attended a service for one. But at Seattle's funeral, those
whites from all around Puget Sound who saw him for
the great and prophetic leader he was gathered together
with the people of the tribes he ruled to show their
respect. It was a wonderfully rich occasion: a Catholic
funeral said by a Native American priest, followed by
one of the tribesmen who, in the measured cadence used

in tribal burials down through the centuries, recited the great events of Seattle's life.

A plaque was erected in his honor—and then Chief Seattle was largely forgotten, as the people of his tribes were largely dispatched from history. But there was something about this great man that would not be forgotten. He had counseled peace when others wanted war. He had warned against the white man's prideful expansion, and forecast what contaminating the environment would yield.

His majestic words proved to be painfully correct.

When the modern ecological movement began to grow in America and throughout Europe, it was not surprising that Seattle quickly became one of its patron saints. He had taught that the earth was family to be loved and cherished, not an enemy to be conquered and exploited. Even as injustice was wrought upon him and his people, he stood for principles that were right then and live on today—with even more urgency.

Buerge, David M., "The Man We Call Seattle," in *The Washingtonians: A Biographical Portrait of the State,* ed. by David Brewster and David M. Buerge, Sasquatch Books, Seattle, WA, 1988.

V. Making
a Stand

Georges Bernanos

Dag Hammarskjöld

Thomas More

Edith Stein

Georges Bernanos

Daily needs and lofty dreams. How often they are in conflict. We want so badly to go here or to do that, but are held back by the nagging necessities of life. Georges Bernanos suffered the indignities of not having all his worldly needs met, but he was after something far more important.

GEORGES BERNANOS was having a rough time of it. Again.

It was the mid-1930s; he had been forced to leave his home in France, the landlord selling off his furniture and books to recoup unpaid rent. He had six children, and a wife with tuberculosis. A recent motorcycle accident had left him a cripple; he needed two canes to walk. Things had gotten so bad that instead of waiting until he had a part of a book finished, Bernanos was sending off a few dozen pages at a time to get money from his publisher. It was a nightmare to hear his children and wife screaming at him each morning, "Your pages, Papa! Your pages!"

Fame had come early for Bernanos, but what followed were too many years of books and articles that simply could not support his family. He had stubbornly held to his vision of writing as a vocation, not a way of making money. In the midst of an agnostic, skeptical, materialistic era, he insisted on placing his characters on a battlefield of right and wrong to "work out their salvation or their doom with a truth which is beyond analysis and in a dimension of belief which the reader may not possess," his biographer concluded. He was deep in writing a murder mystery that his publisher thought might rescue, if not his reputation, at least his financial wellbeing. But Bernanos couldn't keep his mind on making the money he needed.

Bernanos couldn't develop a plot for his main character—a priest/detective who was actually a masquerading woman. Another character—this one a man—kept pushing into his imagination as he sat writing in yet another of the string of barely furnished homes, this one in Majorca. He could see this character so well: a frail priest in a tiny French village. He was a fervent soul and he tried hard, but the Cure Ambricourt was a miserable failure at the job of inspiring the people of his tiny parish. His people thought him a drinker, a fool. He was dying, and so disorganized that he kept putting off seeing a doctor.

Hardly the stuff of a potential best seller. But when Bernanos' *The Diary of a Country Priest* appeared in 1936, the French—and soon, with the many translations that followed people throughout the world—knew he had taken them on a journey deep into a man's soul. A classic had been published that would insure Bernanos' place in literature, telling as it did with unremitting fidelity the daily life of man dedicated to God who was constantly being pulverized in the crucible of his daily work. Although the face and features of the country priest were never revealed (we never even learn his name), few who have read the book do not clearly have in mind his or her own Cure. It is a face torn by self-doubt, suffering, wondering. And yet it is the face of kindness and perseverance. How many, in reading this book, have not felt themselves to be the country priest, trying so hard to do the right thing, failing more times than succeeding, misunderstood.

Journal d'un Cure de Campagne was not and is not an easy book to read. The groaning of this priest's soul is heard on virtually every page, his self-doubt achingly evident, his end all too predictable. It is a painful book; a half dozen pages at one reading is about all anyone can endure. But it was pure Bernanos: a reflection of a man who spent a lifetime trying to figure out how the mysteries of God interact with the ways of mankind. And so many memorable passages from the book are choice morsels that can be plucked from the table Bernanos has set, ever-sustaining nourishment for a person's spiritual journey.

Bernanos' literary career started with a narrow focus —he was a right-wing Catholic and a staunch royalist, quite willing to rail against this foolishness called democracy, against the Jews, against Protestants and foreigners corrupting his venerable France. He wrote for the daily newspaper of *Action francaise,* demonstrated in the streets, a righteous young man sure of his convictions. It was a time in France when the old order resisted the new. Social change and political reform were in the air. Bernanos and his Church stood rigidly firm against progressive forces.

With the horrible slaughter of World War I—and the aftermath of hate, profiteering, and false gaiety—Bernanos began a process that would mold him into a much broader thinker and writer. He would always be impassioned, angry at injustice and cruelty; but he came to see that there was something more important than the ebbs and flows of political movements. More important, he saw that the Church he was so devoted to could be a formidable oppressor, identifying not with the poor and the scorned but with its rich and powerful supporters. Once he had completed his university work, Bernanos felt compelled to write about the inner workings of good and evil; but soon he was a father of an ever-growing family, and took a job as insurance inspector. So, on trains and in cafes and hotels, he began work on a novel.

Under the Sun of Satan, published in 1926, was the first of eight novels Bernanos would write, but it clearly pointed the direction that his fictional works would take and featured the first of the many priests who would be frequent main characters.

In *Under the Sun of Satan,* the reader is swept into the life of a young priest, Donissan, a modern day Cure d'Ars. But even in his holiness, he is constantly tempted. Bernanos in bold strokes informs the reader that it is not merely other mortals or happenstance, but indeed Satan himself, who is involved. One night Donissan became lost and a friendly fellow traveler seems to encourage

him. Only slowly does Donissan realize his companion is
Satan himself—and when Donissan draws the man closer
to get a good look at him, he sees his own face. A child
dies, and Donissan is prevailed upon to raise him, and
indeed the child, held up to a crucifix, does seem to open
his eyes. But is it Satan or God who is at work? A young
girl, made pregnant by a nobleman, kills him and takes
another lover; about to die, she is transported by Donissan to the church, so she can die in God's presence. For
this, the priest is judged imprudent and is sent to do
penance in a monastery. The scene of Donissan's self-
flagellation is relentless and riveting.

This was the time of the Roaring 20s in America, and
of wholesale debauchery in Europe and suddenly a
writer burst upon the scene telling readers they lived
under the sun of Satan, the evil one who never rested,
who wanted their allegiance and their souls and could
strike fancy bargains in the process. Bernanos was talking about redemption, salvation, damnation. Readers
were left breathless by the book; Bernanos was an overnight success. He not only demonstrated great literary
skill; he conveyed spiritual validity as well. He quit the
insurance business and devoted himself full time to writing.

Throughout this and subsequent novels, the forces of
good and evil do battle; actions springing from the best
of intentions not only go awry, but bring pain and suffering to the innocent. Few of the books were successful; there were desperate periods when Bernanos had
barely enough to care for his family. But he was relentless, even if his message was not always well received.
Unless the work was brilliant, morality proved a diffi-

cult quality to purvey. Yet Bernanos had shown a special knack for entering the mind and heart of priests —he, a layman and the father of a large family. His body of work was so powerful (although not always profitable) that he was called the French Dostoevsky.

In his fiction he could draw back from the real world and paint impressionistic portraits of men and women caught in the currents of life, showing natural and supernatural forces bombarding their bodies and souls. But there was another side of Bernanos, often forgotten. His essays and journalistic work covered a period when few European writers could see clearly the ramification of the events that were shaking the world.

Bernanos' eye was unfailing. Because of his powerful pen, he would later be called the conscience of France. While his beloved Catholic Church condoned the holy crusade of the Spanish Civil War—pitting as it did Christianity against communism—Bernanos saw it for what it was. There was no compassion on either side, no God; merely men wanting to impose their will, setting aside decency in the name of either "order" or "revolution." The Communists committed atrocities; Franco's forces slaughtered helpless elderly and children. Bernanos looked for honor within his Church and did not find it: on Majorca, where he lived, if a citizen could not produce a document proving that he had received the sacraments at Easter, he could be shot as a Communist.

When the Munich Pact promised peace, when the French and Petain handed their destiny over to Hitler in return for indentured servitude, Bernanos rose up to call his people to account for their cowardice. DeGaulle credited Bernanos as one of the great inspirations that sustained the French Resistance. Even when France celebrated victory over the Nazis at the end of World War II, Bernanos saw the victory as hollow if it did not address what really plagued mankind: armaments, poor distribution of wealth, ultra-nationalism, fanatical religious belief or extreme political philosophy.

War, tyranny, inhumanity raged about him during his lifetime, and he addressed these major issues of his day; but the real understanding of Georges Bernanos—his Rosetta stone, if you will—is still *The Diary of a Country Priest*. A closer look at this giant of spiritual literature is in order.

In January, 1935, Bernanos wrote to a friend about the book he had in mind. He had no idea of a plot, other characters or how the book would end. All he could see was a priest who "will have served God in exact proportion to his belief that he has served Him badly. His naivete will win out in the end, and he will die peacefully of a cancer." Bernanos, like many authors, typically found the process of writing painful; but once he had begun this book, he could hardly wait to get back to it each day.

Bernanos wrote the book in the form of the priest's diary, as the young Cure made his confessions to the pages of his notebook. He begins:

> Mine is a parish like all the rest. They're all alike. Those of today I mean. I was saying so only yesterday . . . that good and evil are probably evenly distributed, but on such a low plain, very low in-

deed! Or if you like they lie one over the other; like oil and water they never mix.

It becomes quickly apparent that the priest has great difficulty in reaching his parishioners. His sermonettes fall flat, the club he tries to start is a dismal failure, his intentions are constantly mistaken. It is gradually revealed that what might be dismissed as a passing illness or hypochondria is far more serious. The man will die; will he redeem himself and make some impact on his people before he does? A race is on, but page by page, in certain ways, the young priest seems to fall further behind.

He often talks with the Cure de Torcy, an older and more shrewd priest, who constantly admonishes this idealistic cleric on the realities of life and people:

If ever you glimpse the passing truth, take a good look at her, so as to be quite sure you'll know her again; but don't expect her to make eyes at you. Gospel truth makes eyes at nobody.

There is a certain battle going on between these men as each seeks his sanctity. Various critics have been certain Bernanos saw himself as the cure de Torcy, while others adamantly maintain he was embodied in the young country priest. Surely, though, he is both. In the case of each man, mysticism and holiness is grounded in real and mundane events. Each grasps to hold on to his faith, to be honest in looking at himself.

The young country priest tries to reach out to God and there is no consolation:

Georges Bernanos

Never have I made such efforts to pray, at first calmly and steadily, then with a kind of savage, concentrated violence, till at last, having struggled back into calm with a huge effort, I persisted, almost desperately (desperately! How horrible it sounds!) in a sheer transport of will which set me shuddering with anguish. Yet—nothing.

But the reader can clearly see this is far from a hopeless life; while his faith might falter, the events in the parish seem calculated to bring him low, and the people can be often bitter and immovable, his faith illuminates him in the darkest hours, redeeming and renewing him:

Too often one would suppose, to hear us talk, that we Catholics preached a Spiritualists' Deity, some vague kind of Supreme Being in no way resembling the Risen Lord we have learnt to know as a marvelous and living friend, who suffers our pain, takes joy in our happiness, will share our last hour and receive us into His arms, upon His heart.

In his defeats, he triumphs because he will not give in—not to the forces of evil, not to his own fatigue at fighting the good fight each hour and day of his life. How will he deal with a mother who hates God after the loss of an infant son? What to do when the student he thinks is the best and most attentive tells him it is his eyes that captivate her? It is a grounded mysticism, with no easy epiphanies.

Bernanos lived the same way, not allowing an early fame to shape the kind of writing he would do, but listen-

217

ing to that inner voice which constantly prodded him on. His wife and children, justly concerned about their daily bread, may have called out to him for the "pages," but on those pages had to be something that mattered, that would reveal something of the way God works in each human being, in the world's events. Bernanos saw himself in the company of those who, like the country priest, were "Madmen stretching our hands to clasp the moon reflected in water."

After devoting himself to writing about and to his country both during and after World War II, Bernanos again turned to fiction, for what would be his last work. He was asked to write the script for a proposed movie on the execution by guillotine of a group of 18th century Carmelite nuns during the French Revolution. It is a supreme irony that his work was found unacceptable—rejected, in effect—and only surfaced after his death in 1948. *Dialogues of the Carmelites* was eventually set to music by Francis Poulenc, performed at La Scala, and then throughout the world—a haunting testimony to the abuse of civil authority and the power that remains with those true to themselves.

Yet *The Diary of a Country Priest* remained Bernanos' favorite and most famous work. He paid it a high compliment: "I love it as if someone else had written it." And Bernanos' biographer, Robert Speaight, concludes that the book has endured because, "If the face of the *cure de campagne* was to remain so vividly and affectionately in the reader's mind, one reason may have been that, in the nature of the case, Bernanos had been unable to describe it. But we should easily recognize it if we met along the road or even, maybe, at times, in the mirror."

Georges Bernanos

Bernanos, George, *The Diary of A Country Priest,* Macmillan Paperbacks Edition, New York, 1962.

Bush, William, *Georges Bernanos,* Twayne, New York, 1969.

Hebblewaite, Peter, *Bernanos: An Introduction,* Hillary House Publications, New York, 1965.

Speaight, Robert, *Georges Bernanos: A Biography,* Liveright, New York, 1974.

Dag Hammarskjöld

How difficult it is to take your beliefs into the workplace. Harder still to do it without preaching or moralizing. Dag Hammarskjöld, an internationally acclaimed diplomat, approached his work with a simplicity and honesty that, while it might have been misunderstood and didn't always produce the desired end result, was unfailingly authentic.

T HE SPRING and summer months of 1961 marked one of the most dismal periods in the otherwise distinguished career of Dag Hammarskjöld. During his eight years as secretary-general of the United Nations, Hammarskjöld had managed—with a combination of brilliant political acumen, Job-like patience, and the consistent employment of a towering personal integrity

Dag Hammarskjöld

the UN hadn't yet witnessed in its young life—to bring peace to scores of trouble spots around the world.

But his past accomplishments could not mask the present reality: the latest initiative, in the Congo, had deteriorated into a bloodbath. Innocent United Nations peace keepers had been killed, atrocities were being reported almost daily, high-sounding agreements were made and immediately broken. And the secretary-general was being personally derided as a murderer and a lackey of Western imperialism. A long list of otherwise friendly countries, from France to Morocco to Brazil, lined up to condemn him.

As the plane carrying Hammarskjöld and his staff made its approach on a September night to the airport at Ndola, in what is now Zambia, and then flew off, people on the ground were somewhat relieved he wasn't landing there after all. It was no pleasure to have to contend with Hammarskjöld in such troubled times. He was a stiff, tense, aloof idealist, never satisfied to let warring factions work out their differences in the age-old ways, always wanting to talk, unwilling to agree to the behind-the-scenes deals that made international diplomacy possible. And this time he was coming to meet a renegade Congolese leader with nothing in hand, no grand plan, simply presenting himself "naked to my enemies." Such romanticism was not the currency of African politics.

At Ndola, they turned off the runway lights and went to bed. Even after a brilliant flash illuminated the Western sky, no one took immediate action. Morning was soon enough to locate the impatient Mr. Hammarskjöld.

When the crash site was reached the next day and

221

Hammarskjöld's body found—his hand clutching a clump of grass in a last, desperate grasp for life—local officials scrambled to lay blame elsewhere. It was pilot error, enemy ground fire, sabotage, a dramatic suicide aboard the plane. It was anybody's fault but theirs. But even the pettiness of those he was coming to help, running from him even in death, could not blunt the international reaction. Only in his absence was Hammarskjöld's true worth felt. The world knew it had lost a great man.

How great this man had been, and with what pure motives he had lived his life, would be elucidated a few years later when the thoughts he had entrusted only to the pages of his diary were published. *Markings* is the unique, eloquently honest journal of a man—a seasoned diplomat who had mediated between disparate parties throughout his life—who had also taken time to record ". . . my negotiations with myself and with God." Not often is a soul so exposed as is Hammarskjöld's in *Markings*. What is even rarer is that a person with so prominent and powerful a position, so public a face, would be revealed as so vulnerable a mortal, numbed by loneliness, struggling with his faith, agonizing over his shortcomings, trying to live by principles that were constantly mocked, defied and challenged. And rarer still, his acknowledgment of the faith that sustained him, the eternal force that empowered him to do his work on a troubled planet.

Markings is an incandescent look into the inner life of a man who always sought compromise, but found he could never compromise himself. These incisive moments of reflection on a life's journey introduce us to a self-important young man who boasts:

> Life only yields to the conqueror. Never accept what can be gained by giving in. You will be living off stolen goods, and your muscles will atrophy.

. . . to the outwardly successful government official who laments:

> Time goes by; reputation increases, ability declines.

. . . to the seeker who cries out in his darkness and agony:

> Pray that your loneliness may spur you into finding something to live for, great enough to die for.

. . . to one enlightened, finally *seeing,* who exalts:

> In a dream I walked with God through the deep places of creation; past walls that receded and gates that opened, through hall after hall of silence, darkness and refreshment—the dwelling place of souls acquainted with light and warmth—until, around me, was an infinity into which we all flowed together and lived anew, like the rings made by raindrops falling upon wide expanses of calm dark waves.

. . . to the mature spirit who measures himself by the strictest standards:

> If you fail, it is God, thanks to your having betrayed Him, who will fail mankind. You fancy you

can be responsible to God: can you carry the responsibility *for* God?

. . . and finally to the sage who understands:

Do not seek death. Death will find you. But seek the road which makes death a fulfillment.

Your body must become familiar with its death —in all its possible forms and degrees—as a self-evident, imminent, and emotionally neutral step on the way towards the goal you have found worthy of your life.

Dag Hammarskjöld was a most unlikely candidate to be such a pilgrim of the spirit. He was born into a family of privilege that professed high ethical standards. For centuries, his wealthy forebears had been honored members of Sweden's civil service aristocracy; indeed, not long after Dag's birth in 1905, his father was appointed prime minister of the Swedish government. The obligation to serve country and fellow man was in the marrow of the Hammarskjöld men. When a particularly difficult problem arose in the Swedish government, "Try one of the Hammarskjölds" was often the solution.

In college, Dag seemed well-suited for a career in government. He was attractive in a non-threatening, plain sort of way, an outstanding student, upstanding, diligent and scrupulous—perhaps to a fault, the only hint that just being as decent a man as those before him would not be enough. Especially among college students —then in the vanguard of the radical de-Christianization which would sweep over Sweden—he was considered likable, but much too bent on perfectionism; a likable prig. He was one of those purposeful young men who are admired and respected, but certainly not loved. On Saturday nights, when his classmates went out dancing, Hammarskjöld studied. He enjoyed the company of young men and women, but seemed to require the company of neither.

No one had any idea of the spiritual storm gathering within him, the inner voice that was neither guide nor sustenance at that time of his life, only a torment. On those rare occasions when he felt alone and driven to talk about his reading of Thomas a Kempis or Buber or Marcel, about the spiritual and metaphysical dimensions of life, his classmates greeted his openness with blank stares. He did not persist.

His rise through the civil service ranks was meteoric; his capacity for work, boundless. Although he felt hollow and aimless, Hammarskjöld was regarded as among Sweden's best and brightest. In 1952, his brilliant career was advanced handsomely when, after only a year as vice chairman, he was asked at the age of 47 to head the Swedish delegation to the United Nations. In a job that called for—in addition to the more serious responsibilities—an everpresent smile, entertaining cocktail party patter and daily glad-handing, Hammarskjöld was sadly out of place. Few people remember him from his early days in New York, his was such a forgettable face, a personality so bland. In those corridors of influence at the United Nations, in the fashionable drawing rooms of the powerful, Dag Hammarskjöld was a nonentity.

When he was named the UN's second secretary general in 1953, it was not because anyone felt strongly about his abilities or moral fiber. No one saw within him the person who would give the office the credibility and stature it so sorely needed as the United Nations struggled to make the world believe it mattered.

He was a compromise choice who came into office after candidates from Canada, Belgium, the Philippines and India—each well-known and respected—were rejected by the Soviet Union. Moscow wanted someone neutral—and ineffectual. It was fully expected that Dag Hammarskjöld's administration would be uneventful, as colorless as the man no one knew well enough to distrust. Observers concluded that any hopes the UN might have to become a strong presence in world affairs would have to wait until the end of his term.

Hammarskjöld took on what his predecessor Trygve Lie called "the most difficult job in the world," becoming a leader who represented neither a nation nor an ideological coalition. He commanded no armies and could expect no one's allegiance. He could expect and would have to weather continual misunderstanding, suspicion, contempt and insults. He was an easy and visible target, with no built-in political constituency; no one had "elected" him. Few even knew his name. He stood for nothing more than an abstraction new to the world: the international community. As the symbol of such an amorphous dream, his only source of influence would be himself.

It was laughable. What could a faceless, colorless man, with what others called a "devastating impersonality," accomplish in a world—and in a world organization—that responded to charismatic leadership and raw power?

He seemed exactly wrong for his post. And, in a way,

he knew it. But in the year he was named secretary general, Dag Hammarskjöld reached a turning point in his life. The loneliness that had haunted him had also prepared him; that deep, dark hole, the hunger within him, his own pain had disposed Hammarskjöld to feel also the agony of the peoples of this earth. And the inner voice that had throbbed inside his head—loud, insistent but unclear—now was clarified. He was no longer working alone. He uttered—and meant—a single word:

I don't know who—or what—put the question, I don't know when it was put. I don't even remember answering. But at some moment I did answer *Yes* to Someone—or Something—and from that hour I was certain that existence is meaningful and that, therefore, my life, in self-surrender, had a goal.

From that moment I have known what it means 'not to look back,' and 'to take no thought for the morrow.'

. . . I came to a time and place where I realized that the Way leads to a triumph which is a catastrophe, and to a catastrophe which is a triumph, that the price for committing one's life would be reproach, and that the only elevation possible to man lies in the depths of humiliation. After that, the word 'courage' lost its meaning, since nothing could be taken from me.

"Humiliation?" "Catastrophe?" "Reproach?" "Self-surrender?"

Not the vocabulary of the influential of this earth, but to Hammarskjöld those words were at the very core of

227

his reason to be alive. In an Edward R. Murrow radio interview, Hammarskjöld told of the two rivers that converged in him:

From generations of soldiers and government officials on my father's side I inherited a belief that no life was more satisfactory than one of selfless service to your country—or humanity. . . . From scholars and clergymen on my mother's side I inherited a belief that . . . all men were equals as children of God, and should be met and treated by us as our masters.

Fired by this inner vision and blessed with an unbelievable stamina that allowed him to go weeks at a time with but a few hours sleep each night, Hammarskjöld embarked on a mission of global peace-making perhaps unparalleled in history in its scope.

He flew to Peking to gain the release of imprisoned American airmen, and traveled to the Middle East to defuse the crisis in Lebanon and Jordan and to keep the issue of a free Palestine from erupting into war. Hungary, Cambodia, Thailand, Egypt—when trouble occurred, the secretary general was on a plane, or on a phone or cabling his readiness to intercede, to find some shred of commonality, anything to delay or avoid armed combat. In an inspired move, he made the weight of the UN felt during the Suez crisis by creating the multinational United Nations Emergency Force that helped clear the Suez Canal, returning it to peaceful use and avoiding further bloodshed. Warring nations were flabbergasted—and literally disarmed—to have troops in their presence whose only mission was *not* to fight. Such

Dag Hammarskjöld

a concept had never been employed before. And at Hammarskjöld's death, UN forces in the Congo were preventing a bad situation from becoming worse.

Perhaps Hammarskjöld's most lasting accomplishment was his work on behalf of the dozens of economically underdeveloped and newly independent countries in Asia and Africa emerging from centuries of colonial rule to take their place in the community of nations. He was affectionately called "the custodian of the brushfire peace." Hammarskjöld saw clearly that these impoverished new nations, with no history of self-government, and with few citizens trained in medicine, economics, business or agriculture, needed the alternatives only the United Nations might provide, as statesmen of various ideologies were vying to envelop them in their spheres of power.

Each time a conflict threatened or fighting erupted, Hammarskjöld did as most mediators: he looked objectively at the situation and tried to get as many informed points of view as possible. Then he forced himself to erase his personal preferences and dislikes, the bombast and threats that had been exchanged, the attendant depravity and corruption. Thus purified, he tried to imagine himself in the position of each of the parties involved. What harsh winds had brought them to this point? What did the drumbeats of their hearts tell them? What did they want? What did they *need?* Regardless of how they were portrayed in the media, what were these people really like? If their borders had been violated, what of their souls? What injustices had they suffered that they could not tolerate? What would it take to restore their personal honor and dignity?

Companions Along the Way

During those golden days of the United Nations, leaders of nations deep in bitter conflict could sense they were dealing with a man of unassailable principle, one they could trust, one who truly had their best interests at heart. And then, so often, the rectitude of this man, his mere presence in their country—the humble, broken way he looked at them with his deep blue eyes—imposed an unspoken moral obligation to make peace.

In a world given to suspicion and distrust, here was a man that each side could feel was on *their* side.

In *Markings,* Hammarskjöld points to his inspiration:

> Jesus' 'lack of moral principles?' He sat at meals with publicans and sinners, he consorted with harlots. Did he do this to obtain their votes? Or did he think that, perhaps, he could convert them by such 'appeasement?' Or was his humanity rich and deep enough to make contact, even in them, with that in human nature which is common to all men, indestructible, and upon which the future has to be built?

His inner life empowered his public life as *Markings* so clearly shows, but Hammarskjöld kept the two so separate that not once in his diary does he ever mention what was going on in the world or in his work. And, conversely, in the public arena, he never once wagged a moralistic, righteous finger at anyone. For him, the dual commitment was mandatory; he had to unite in one life the *via activa* and the *via contemplativa.* As he wrote in one of his "negotiations" with himself, "In our era, the road to holiness necessarily passes through the world of action."

Dag Hammarskjöld

As central as this tenet was to him, he could never ask others to live or think as he did; he could never *preach* ethical, compassionate behavior. All he could do was struggle to live it as best he could, and by his example, encourage others to do the same.

Lest the impression come through that Hammarskjöld was some sort of sop, a weak fish happy and willing to be arbitrarily devoured by the shark of the moment, it is important to be clear that is not at all who he was. He was an accomplished economist—one of the first to use and understand the term "planned economy"—widely read in world history and literature, an extremely effective administrator who oversaw some 4,000 Secretariat employees and a pragmatist who was equally impatient with world-weary cynicism as he was with foolish optimism.

And though he talked of humiliation and self-surrender, he was extremely thin-skinned about criticism and possessed a towering ego. Who but a man with a great sense of his place and his worth could be so bold as to not only with to be responsible *to* God, but carry the burden *for* God? When *Markings* appeared he was castigated for his vanity; he was called a blasphemer who envisioned himself *too much* as the Man he tried to emulate. In *Markings,* Hammarskjöld was clear about his aspirations:

With the love of Him Who knows all,
With the patience of Him Whose now is eternal,
With the righteousness of Him Who has never
   failed,
With the humility of Him Who has suffered all the
   possibilities of betrayal.

Companions Along the Way

A haiku verse he wrote says it succinctly:

Denied any outlet
The heat transmuted
The coal into diamonds.

Hammarskjöld knew his demons. He was ambitious, arrogant and cold; he could affect a boyish charm when it served his purposes, or dismiss with a flicker of his eyes. But, as the haiku so clearly states, he gave himself no outlet, would not settle for an accommodating embrace of his foibles, the exhausted compromise that many great men and women forge with their deepest yearnings.

After his death, as hagiographers began to obscure the flesh and blood Hammarskjöld, he was hailed as a great man of the church. This is revisionist piety; he was nothing of the sort. While Hammarskjöld was not a church-goer, he was a frequent church visitor. Rarely did he travel to a city and not stop at one of its churches, temples or mosques. At the United Nations he turned a tiny space on the ground floor into a meditation room. There in a bare room—containing only a massive block of Swedish iron, illuminated by a single shaft of light —Hammarskjöld could often be seen during the day. There, he sought the inspiration and insights that sheaves of briefing papers, eyewitness accounts, a superior intellect, even unquestionable altruism could not yield. He walked the narrow path of peace; he needed constant guidance. He felt deeply that the United Nations reached beyond the temporal order into the eternal and he knew that if he didn't take time to restate that to

Dag Hammarskjöld

himself, to go back to the eternal source, the power that sustained him would be gone.

Dag Hammarskjöld, this Christian mystic who practiced his beliefs in a most unlikely and profoundly secular setting, has had a lasting effect both on the country of his birth and the world at large. When it was published, *Markings* shocked Sweden, where Christianity was considered a foolish museum piece, an intellectually dishonest pursuit at best. Here was a man with a *living* faith that was the basis for a most productive and honorable career. It could not be disregarded. His life and death and the posthumous publication of his thoughts were nothing short of an epoch-making spiritual event. Today Swedish schoolchildren commit his poems to memory, his single volume is already a classic in the country's literature.

And for the rest of the world, as Hammarskjöld's life is examined, it is difficult to look at the shimmering, pale green United Nations building, rising up, alone and aloof, along the East River in New York, and not think about the man. For, since his day, the UN has yet to regain the might wielded by the hand of a true peace maker. As nation rises up against nation, faction against faction, as vitriolic speeches echo in the great General Assembly hall, as death marches across television screen and printed page, a longing sets in for this great companion.

Aulen, Gustaf, *Dag Hammarskjöld's White Book: The Meaning of "Markings,"* Fortress Press, Philadelphia, PA, 1969.

Companions Along the Way

Hammarskjöld, Dag, *Markings,* Knopf, New York, 1964.

Stolpe, Sven, *Dag Hammarskjöld: A Spiritual Portrait,* (Eng. translation by Naomi Walford), Scribners, New York, 1966.

Van Dusen, Henry Pitney, *Dag Hammarskjöld: The Statesman and His Faith,* 1967.

Thomas More

Often we wonder: Is the work we do worthwhile? Or are we willingly contributing to a system, institution or company that is intrinsically corrupt? The life of Thomas More will help to address that question, which crops up time and time again in everyone's life. For Thomas More was a man who seemed on both sides of many issues, yet held onto a personal integrity that makes him one of the most fascinating—and perplexing—men in history.

T HE CHURCH in which Thomas More grew up was corrupt and venal. Cardinals and bishops were wealthy landowners who kept serfs in poverty and their mistresses in splendor. The papacy itself was more of a political battleground than a religious refuge. The pope (or *popes*—there were two at times) was often viewed as more of a greedy prince than a universal pastor. Bribery, warfare, intrigue and assassination went along with one, holy, Catholic and apostolic. Alexander VI, who reigned from More's boyhood well into his manhood, is popularly considered one of the worst—if not *the* worst—pope.

In his best-known book, *Utopia,* More wrote of a land where there were but few laws governing the affairs of her citizens, where people could choose to honor their God in any matter befitting them and divorce was possible on easy grounds.

And yet he was later to become England's chief law officer, proved to be a staunch defender of his faith against Martin Luther—to the point of executing heretics—and was himself put to death because he would not violate the integrity of the Church by sanctioning the divorce of a king to whom he had sworn his loyalty.

Confusing? Will the real Thomas More stand up?

To be sure, this Companion went through many, many seasons in his life. And the period in which he lived —1478 to 1535—is strikingly similar to our own times. In More's day anticlericalism was at its zenith and the best young men went into law—for a surety in an age of unsureness, to earn a good living and perhaps catapult them into politics.

Thomas was born into the family of John More, a moderately wealthy lawyer, who was eager for his son to follow in his profession. The young More went to the best schools—including Oxford—and eventually was admitted to the bar. While he did well enough in his legal training, his was an inquiring mind that ranged from astronomy to the classics; he loved Latin and Greek. He was searching for more than just a future as a wealthy lawyer.

While this was an age of turmoil within England, as royal houses battled for primacy and the Tower of London witnessed the death of more than one monarch, it was also a fertile time of discovery and rediscovery. Christopher Columbus had sailed to America and a new school of thinking was reclaiming the ancient classics of the Greeks and Romans that had been pushed aside by the emphasis on technical and logical studies—scholasticism—that flourished in the later Middle Ages. Called "humanists," these thinkers sought not to replace religious values with secular ones, but to take the best of the Old World and apply it to the New. Erasmus, a leader of the humanists, was a friend and correspondent of Thomas More.

The dualism in Thomas More's life was immediately apparent in his early years as a grown man. He enjoyed the perquisites afforded him in the practice of law and yet he spent time in the austere, silent London charterhouse of the Carthusians, one of the few religious groups that had not given in to the corruption and ease of the day. He loved fine clothes and adornments of gold but often he wore a hairshirt beneath. While he thought about being a priest, he admitted his flesh was too weak to honor a vow of celibacy and he married.

If he could not be a priest, Thomas More vowed he would be as devout a layman as he could in the secular world of his day.

Thomas More was certainly a young man on the rise

and in the year 1515 was given an important commission: to negotiate the king's treaty concerning the trade of cloth and wool. During the months in Flanders that it took to complete his work, More found himself with much time on his hands and, being a man who considered wasted time next to a sin, he set about writing a book to express his thoughts not on what was, but what might be. Upon completing the book, More pondered whether or not it should be published, for it seemed so at odds with what he was coming to stand for.

In the book, More coined a word for an ideal kingdom—Utopia—which, interestingly enough, literally translates as "no such place." It was a place where jewels were given to the children as playthings, men and women were priests, work was shared by all and the harvest was distributed according to need, not station in life. There was no such a thing as private property and homes were changed every ten years. In More's Utopia, there was no need for courtly manners, for there was neither royalty nor subjects. And there was no need for many laws, for what was there to protect? Religious expression depended on a person's desires; unworkable marriages could be dissolved and if people were so ill that they wanted to end their life, assistance would be given to speed their death.

In *Utopia,* the issue of entering public service is hotly contested. It mirrored the debate that went on in More's day between humanists like Erasmus, who felt that scholars who worked within the royal court would only be corrupted, and those who argued that service to the king was a noble and religious calling of its own. And, it was a conflict that raged in More's mind, for he knew

Thomas More

the Flanders assignment might easily lead to an appointment on king's council.

More had designed an ideal kingdom and soon after the call came from King Henry VIII for him to labor in a real one. Was it raw ambition or the desire of a righteous man to have some influence in the government of his country? Or, like many issues in Thomas More's life, was there some—perhaps equal parts—of each? He knew that the court and the system supporting it was corrupt, and yet he chose to become involved in it.

With this appointment, the stakes were significantly raised in Thomas More's life. He was no longer an obscure functionary, but a rising official at the center of power. He was about to take an active part in the kind of base and unscrupulous society he had so brilliantly satirized in *Utopia*.

More proved to be an indispensible councillor and was a favorite of the king. Henry would often send for him not only to discuss public affairs, but to tap More's vast knowledge of science, philosophy and theology. More won favor not only with this intelligence but with a wonderful sense of humor. His lawyer's training and the disciplines of rhetoric, grammar and elegant speech that the humanists espoused had not blotted out his ability to laugh and make puns—both on himself and others. Noting that he was becoming an admired man, More said of the stories that circulated about him: "A tale that fleeth through many mouths catcheth many new feathers." He believed neither in fawning nor in stupidity and, as one biographer wrote of him, "More was never more witty than when he was least amused."

More proved to be an effective liaison between the

239

king—who rarely attended Council meetings—and Cardinal Wolsey, the Lord Chancellor, who presided at the Council, made policy and was the most powerful man in English politics. Both men trusted More—and such trust, within a court where conniving, bribery and infighting were the standard and raw ambition was a given, was remarkable.

More's role in the politics and legislation of the day was a mix of addressing the repugnant and the altruistic. He had to help raise taxes so that the Christian ruler of England could stay at war with the Christian ruler of France, but he was also able to reduce the power of the clergy and to bring justice within the reach of the poor.

After some ten years in England's service, the dissatisfaction of two men with the status quo began to configure the years ahead for Thomas More. King Henry VIII had grown tired of Catherine his queen, who had not produced a male heir to the throne. And an Augustinian monk, Martin Luther, could no longer be bound to a Church whose primate offered indulgences for sale, whose sacraments no longer made sense to him, and which had undermined the role of faith as a pathway to salvation.

Cardinal Wolsey proved ineffective in obtaining Henry's annulment from the Vatican so that he might marry Anne Boleyn, and Thomas More was asked to become Lord Chancellor. It was a unique appointment, as More had never sought the chancellorship and would be moreover the first layman within memory to serve in the office. He knew the quagmire that faced him, but Henry promised that he would not be dragged into the matter of who would be the queen of England.

Thomas More

To More, the heresy of Martin Luther was a corruption that had first to be stamped out, less souls be lost and civil discord sweep over Europe. He vigorously wrote tracts defending the faith and refuting Luther. This was certainly not the world of Utopia, but a real world where there was but one expression of Christian beliefs—at least in More's mind—through the Catholic Church.

While the threat of these so-called "protestants" was a major concern, Henry was more troubled with who would occupy his bedroom. Henry successfully browbeat scholars at European universities to side with him and it was More's task to present these coerced findings to Parliament before they were forwarded on to Rome. As Henry moved still further—asserting that he, not the pope, had jurisdiction over the English clergy—More could take no more. He quietly resigned his office and thus began the war between these two men which eventually would lead to the scaffold.

To marry Ann Boleyn and take control of the clergy, Henry VIII did not need the sanction of a man he could appoint or dismiss from office, but he hungered for his approval. More, who had been a scrupulously honest judge in an era when bribe-taking was commonplace, stood for something beyond the law of the land and Henry wanted More's moral seal affixed to his actions. Henry had passed an act regulating the succession to the throne and virtually all his subjects and the English clergy readily swore a public oath to support it. To refuse was an act of treason, punishable by death and the confiscation of all property.

More was summoned to Lambeth Palace to take his

oath and found himself surrounded by clergymen who were ready to swear and sign. He read the act and as he wrote to his wife Margaret a few days later:

> I showed unto them that my purpose was not to put any fault either in the act or any man that made it, or in the oath or any man that swore it, nor to condemn the conscience of any other man. But as for myself in good faith my conscience so moved me in the matter that, though I would not deny to swear to the succession, yet unto the oath that there was offered to me I could not swear without the jeopardizing of my soul to perpetual damnation.

To More's mind, his king could create for his worldly kingdom any line of succession he pleased, but he could not violate at will his Church's law on divorce. He had always respected the office—be it that of king or pope—regardless of the conduct of the man, but if asked to attest to what his conscience told him was patently wrong, this he could not do.

More's stand drove Henry VIII into a fury. Members of the Royal Court tried to find a way that More could swear to part of the oath. Failing this, they set about to entrap him with the infamous visit of Sir Richard Rich, who would later lie in his testimony that More had denied that Parliament had the power to make Henry VIII the head of the Church of England—a position the king insisted upon, seeing that Rome had not sanctioned his divorce.

His family begged him, his wife raged at him to relent. More lost most of his income in giving up the chancellorship; servants had to be dismissed, and the More family was plunged into what was, for them, poverty. All this turmoil because More, once the king's confidant, had not accepted an oath that, throughout the kingdom, people were swearing. More was an embarrassment to his king and to his family.

During his days in the Tower of London, as the king and his cohorts plotted on what grounds this obstinate man could be tried and dispatched, More wrote *A Dialogue of Comfort Against Tribulation,* which after *Utopia* is the best known among his many books. *Dialogue* is the imaginary conversation between two men on the threat of a painful martyrdom and it obviously mirrors More's interior struggle as he faced a certain death. It is a book from More's heart, drawing on the strength he finds in his faith during this desolate time, yet ever mindful of how fragile is faith and inner resolve, regardless of how strong a person may appear to be.

The story of More's imprisonment and trial is enthralling, both for what he said and for the silence he maintained in the face of the charge of high treason. He neither spoke nor wrote against the king, so he could not rightly be proved treasonous. His majestic silence eloquently underscored the unprincipled actions of his king. More might lose his head, but the mantle of obloquy would remain on the shoulders of his accusers. Choosing his words so carefully, as he always did, he said of the oath:

Of malice, I never spoke anything against it and whatsoever I have spoken on that matter, I have

none otherwise spoken but according to my very
mind, opinion and conscience and for this my taci-
turnity and silence neither your law nor any law in
the world is able justly and rightly to punish me,
unless you may besides lay to my charge either
some word or some fact in deed.

And of his conscience:

This was one of the cases in which I was bounded
that I should not obey my prince . . . in my conscience the truth seemed to be on the other side . . .
wherein I had not informed my conscience neither
suddenly or lightly but by long leisure and diligent
search for the matter. I leave everyman in his conscience and methinketh that in good faith so were
it good conscience every man should leave me to
mine.

Thomas More didn't lose his sense of humor even as
he was taken to his death. The scaffold that held the
block on which he would lay his head was rickety and
ready to fall. Dressed in a coarse servant's gown, his
face now gaunt from months of imprisonment, he turned
to the lieutenant in charge and said, "I pray you Master
Lieutenant, see me safe up, and for my coming down let
me shift for myself."

Many lives and analyses of Thomas More have been
written, most of them congratulatory, some scathing in
their indictments of him as little more than a fawning
careerist who happened to be beheaded. But Thomas
More transcends all these treatments, for he was neither
as perfect nor as calculating as various authors main-

tain. What is powerful about him is that he is, in essence, a saint of the Establishment, a man who had wealth, who worked in the highest ranks of government, and who could have been spared had he only yielded ever so slightly to the winds of his time. He was hardly a wild-eyed mystic or misfit—and, to round out his character, wrote good and lasting books.

More went to his execution because he could not live if he swore allegiance to something his conscience abhorred. But was it a death he courted and wanted? Hardly. As a lawyer, he might have found a way to work around the oath, but he knew that employing his skill to implicitly support a morally bankrupt principle would be merely a contest of intellects. He would not be a player in such a game.

Thomas More haunts us and encourages us to make our stand. He lets us know by his life that the path to goodness is hardly straight and that contradiction is the sign of a thoughtful person who cares enough to think about what they are doing and that inner conflict, given its proper place in a life, leads to right decisions. In an age overtaken by easy secularism, More's life reminds us that one's faith and religious beliefs are not progressive disciplines like mathematics or physics, but need constantly to be reaffirmed to be ready when the moment of testing comes.

Basset, Bernard, *Born for Friendship: The Spirit of Thomas More*, Sheed and Ward, New York, 1965.

Companions Along the Way

Bolt, Robert, *A Man for All Seasons*, Random House, New York, 1962.

Chambers, R.W., *Thomas More*, London, Cape, 1935.

Fox, Alistar, *Thomas More, History and Providence*, Yale University Press, New Haven, CT, 1982.

Kenny, Anthony, *Thomas More*, Oxford University Press, Oxford, 1983.

More, Thomas, *Utopia*, (Paul Turner trans.) Penguin, Baltimore, 1965.

_____, *A Dialogue of Comfort Against Tribulation*, ed. Frank Manley, Yale Univ. Press, New Haven, CT, 1977.

Rupp, Gordon, *Thomas More, The King's Good Servant*, Collins, London, 1978.

Edith Stein

The intellectual life seems to offer the promise of answers to life's questions, but too often the more knowledge we have, the further we get away from the truth. Edith Stein found her answers in the simplest way, and she was transformed.

S HE IS beginning to be called one of the most influential and significant women Europe has produced in our century. The anniversary of her death is honored with television and radio specials; books, periodicals and newspapers throughout the world pay her homage. A postage stamp memorializes her; schools, libraries, streets and community centers bear her name. Strange, isn't it, that an over-sensitive, over-ambitious intellectual, an opinionated, arrogant and rigid young woman would become one of the towering moral beacons of our time?

What makes Edith Stein so inspiring and fascinating is not merely her movement from Judaism to Catholicism, her steadfast courage as she faced a horrible death, her insightful understanding of the new role of woman. It is rather something far deeper, something which underscored everything she did: the amazing integrity with which she lived her life. She allowed no swerving from a path once she found it to be the right one for her —regardless of the difficulties, the pain, the struggle or misunderstanding it might involve. In her study of philosophy, she felt that she had constantly to walk on the edge of an abyss if she were really to grow and learn. Living the considered life constantly brought her to the brink. She never came to conclusions easily or quickly— she was far too intelligent for facile answers—but once something lit up for her, she just went ahead and did it.

There was nothing in her life that she approached halfheartedly, including a search for life's true meaning. And that dogged search carried her from a rich Jewish heritage to the austere cloister of a Catholic convent, through periods of excruciating depression to moments of transcendent clarity, from a firm belief in God to atheism, from a promising career as a philosopher to a Nazi death camp.

Just before Edith Stein and a group of Dutch Jews were to be loaded onto a train for Auschwitz, a solicitous Christian friend, a guard at the Westerbork interment camp, begged to be allowed to intercede. With panic in his eye, he fervently cast about for what he would do; he would call the authorities, see the right official, do something, anything to save her from a certain death. After all, Edith Stein was a Catholic nun. There might be a way. "Why be an exception?" Edith answered calmly. That she was baptized made her no less a Jew. If so many people were suffering in that place, she was not about to retreat to safety, to step back—tempting though it might have been at that moment—from the edge of the abyss.

On an August day in 1942, she was herded into the gas chambers with hundreds of other Jews, standing proudly and serenely until the end as a sacrificial victim for the two great religious faiths she so cherished.

Edith Stein is a worthy Companion along the way because she took all her God-given qualities—the quirks of her personality, her strengths and her weaknesses —faced them head on and did that most difficult of human tasks: forged everything she was into the best possible person she could be. Had she only listened to the praise lavished upon her as a child and student because she was so brilliant, or played upon her moody petulance, Edith Stein might be known today as a fine philosopher, an influential teacher, writer and feminist pioneer, perhaps an eccentric—instead of the spiritual giant that she became.

She was born to an extremely devout German Jewish family in 1891 and quickly developed into a precocious, headstrong little girl. Her older brother, a university student, would carry Edith around the house on his shoulders when she was just four or five, lecturing on Schiller and Goethe and he was continually amazed at how much she understood and could repeat back to him. She was incensed when commanded to attend kindergarten—she knew how intellectually superior she was to her classmates and the foolish activities she would have to endure—and on her sixth birthday pronounced she wanted one gift and no other: to be allowed to attend the "big school."

She was vain, a perfectionist, and when things didn't go her way, or she couldn't prove she was the best and the smartest in everything from reciting poems to participating in adult conversations, she vented her frustration in tears of rage. She bridled when asked to do any housework, reveled when homework was piled on. When her mother braided her hair for school in the morning, Edith would be reading yet another book.

The accepted social roles of men and women, boys and girls at the time made absolutely no sense to her. Even at a young age, only one thing mattered: truth, wherever she found it. And the quest for truth, she was absolutely sure, served both sexes, as well as being equally imposed upon them. She shocked her teachers with a poem written for a class play:

> Let woman equal be with man,
> So loud this suffragette avers,
> In days to come we surely can
> See that a Cab'net Post is hers.

Looking back, it's easy to see why she is called a "brenn," the Yiddish word for "firebrand."

But, within this temperamental, highly complex and competent girl was another, lonely and introverted, confused, unable to assimilate all that her awakening intellect and senses were revealing. Learning excited her to the point of exhaustion. But what was she to do, stop reading? She would sooner die. And when she would see a drunken man on the street or hear an unkind word directed to anyone, it caused her intense pain. Something was very wrong when people were made to suffer; try as she might, she was unable merely to look the other way. In a sense, even as a child, her own body reacted to the suffering in the world by embracing it; she was struck time and time again with inexplicable high fevers after seeing someone else's agony.

Once in school, her thirst for knowledge quickly supplanted the deep religious convictions and practices of the Stein home. She was intoxicated with learning, her mind quickly assimilating what books had to offer and then going off in uncharted directions that astonished her teachers and classmates. But at age 13, the world of facts and ideas suddenly collapsed for Edith. Literally, she had been overwhelmed with this new world that schooling brought. Her childhood faith had been abandoned; there was nothing to hold on to. She teetered on the edge of the abyss before a nervous and physical breakdown forced her to return home.

A severe depression stalked her from age 13 until she was of college age, a period during which Edith Stein also professed atheism. As Judaism had once made ultimate sense to her, the denial of God was now clearly necessary. In her mind, full-scale intellectual and religious lives were impossible, incompatible. God was not something deducible, reasonable or rational and she wanted nothing to do with such a nebulous object.

She was eventually able to return to school and was accepted as one of the first women students at the university at Gottingen. These would be pivotal years for Edith Stein, when she was allowed to study under the gifted Edmund Husserl, the founder of phenomenology. There, in one of Europe's finest institutions of higher learning, where various philosophies and schools of thought battled for acceptance in classrooms and beerhalls, she found herself—against her nihilist, atheistic best intentions—attracted to the brilliant philosopher Max Scheler. A convert from Judaism to Christianity, Scheler talked about a "feeling for values" which broke through all belief systems. He used terms like "the seeing eye" and "the empathetic heart." Only religion made the person completely human, Scheler passionately proclaimed, and only through humility, a loss of one's self in God, would a person ever truly live.

Edith Stein had never heard a professor on a university campus talk quite like that. Humility? What had that ever proved or produced? And, religion! Why was this learned man so taken with religion?

Scheler's concepts remained abstract and untenable until two signal events happened in her life. The first was a visit to the widow of a beloved teacher who had been killed in the war then raging in Europe. As she was making her way to the woman's house, Edith wondered what she would say to the young widow, how she could possibly console her. She knocked on the door, unprepared, empty. When she greeted Edith, the woman's face, rather than being crushed by this tragedy, glowed with hope, a light shown in her eyes from a hidden world Edith Stein as yet knew nothing about.

Edith was not yet about to let one incident, however powerful, invalidate a life carefully constructed through sheer intelligence. But something profound had happened. She had received the intimation of an inner power, a power beyond knowledge, beyond reasoning.

Edith Stein

It was my first encounter with the Cross and divine power that it bestows on those who carry it. For the first time, I was seeing with my very eyes the Church, born from the Redeemer's sufferings, triumphant over the sting of death.

The next transforming experience was hardly as dramatic. In fact, it was so simple that most people would, having experienced it, never remember it had happened.

Edith was visiting the cathedral in Frankfurt—as a tourist, taking in the art and architecture—when a townswoman came in. She was obviously on her way home from the market. She put down her shopping basket, knelt and said a short prayer. Her visit lasted no more than a minute or two, but it struck Edith Stein. She had been immersed in Jewish rituals during her youth and she had attended Protestant services, but this was unique in her experience.

Here was someone coming into the empty church in the middle of a day's work as if to talk with a friend. I have never been able to forget that.

God was surely beckoning her to come closer, but Edith was still not ready to listen, not about to abandon her iron will—the very quality Scheler said a person must leave behind to truly find God. In the ensuing months she passed through her Dark Night of the Soul, feeling listless, unfocused, with "the stillness of death" upon her. She even hoped that on a hike she might fall from a cliff.

Then, at a friend's house, she picked up Teresa of

Avila's *Life*. With her characteristic intensity, Edith read all night. The words of the great mystic pounded at her brain, demanding entrance—and acceptance:

> When God sees that the soul has been flying around for a long time like a bird, seeking him with the intellect, the will and all the other faculties and doing its best to please him, then he rewards it even in this present life. And the reward is so tremendous that a single moment of it is enough to pay the soul for all its earthly sufferings . . . I was so blind! What ever made me think that I could find a remedy apart from you? Such stupidity—running away from the light.

By morning, she said to herself: "This is the truth." The burden had been lifted; she felt alive again.

The next logical step, her conversion to Christianity, was as inevitable to Edith as it was crushing to her family. To them, she was abandoning her faith. To Edith, she was proud to be a Jew—as was Jesus—and now she could embrace him in a fullness a Gentile could never experience. She never flaunted her new beliefs and still attended synagogue with her family, but Edith saw the path she had to take and boldly went on her way.

The years after her baptism saw Edith Stein begin a promising teaching and writing career, and become an acclaimed speaker. She was keenly aware that the individualism of the 19th century was giving way to the social orientation of the 20th and that women would have a new role in the rapidly changing world. She also saw clearly that technology was shrinking the globe and that people were bound together in new ways, for better or worse. World War I had annihilated nations, and in its wake she could already see the great appeal of hyper-nationalism and totalitarianism to ravaged countries like her own. Crowds would come to hear her, often expecting to find a self-important egghead. Instead, there was an attractive unpretentiousness about her that immediately drew her audiences not only to the words, but to the person speaking them. She was well grounded in philosophy and social history; she was also now infused with faith. Edith unabashedly stated that only true religious and moral values could hope to bind and keep people together in that most difficult time—one she intuited would only get worse.

Her talks were wonderfully simple and accessible. She knew that in each person's life there was that germ of goodness that wanted to grow, but so often was undernourished. She spoke especially to the women of her audiences—for the most part still confined to their homes—telling them to find "breathing spaces" during the day.

> God is there [in these moments] and can give us in a single instant exactly what we need. Then the rest of the day can take its course, under the same effort and strain, perhaps, but in peace.

How clearly she saw what today we call "the new woman." It was not enough that they take on a vocation in the world, or become educated or accomplished. As women, they had a distinct charism and responsibility.

> If a woman's vocation is the protection of life and the preservation of the family, she cannot remain

indifferent as to whether or not governments and nations assume forms which are favorable to the growth of the family and the well-being of the young.

In Germany of the early 1930s, the nationalistic fulsomeness to which Edith Stein had alluded in many of her talks began to yield its dreadful fruit. University students randomly and maliciously attacked Jews; the newspapers were filled with virulently anti-Semitic articles; Jewish professors lost their jobs or were refused appointments. A lifelong patriotic German, proud of her Jewish heritage, Edith Stein was stunned. She ached for the centuries-long suffering of her people; she looked back to the great sacrifice of the Cross. She peered into the abyss that was her beloved Germany. She could have simply turned away and emigrated; no one would have ever faulted her for wanting to escape from a country whose moral fabric was unraveling.

Slowly it came to her what she must do. There could be no thought of running away. Somehow—and she did not yet know exactly how—she knew she must, as an individual woman, be ready to stand for both her peoples. In some way, if this agony was to be inflicted, she wanted to be ready to share in the suffering of both Christians and Jews.

She knew well the price and the redemption of suffering—from the ages-old struggle of the Jewish people to know their God, from the sacrifice of Calvary when Christ conquered death and despair with that one triumphant act. Who could know this better than a woman like Edith Stein, steeped in both cultures, both religions?

Edith Stein

But Edith Stein was not a masochist, or a would-be heroine seeking suffering. Sacrifice for its own sake made absolutely no sense to her, besides being intellectually untenable. What did make ultimate sense, in those horrid days, was not to step back from the brink. She must be present as events unfolded in Germany. Regardless.

She had long thought of joining the religious life and finally, at 42—certainly an advanced age to become a postulant—she joined the cloistered order of Carmelites in Cologne. She had held back from the decision, not wanting to further offend her family as she had done with her conversion, but, in her typical fashion, it was now clear what she had to do with her life. It was doubly hard for her to join when she did, in 1933, for the Nazis had finally taken power and persecution of the Jews continued with a new fury. She seemed to be abandoning her family and their beliefs. They were devastated.

As her later life was to show, it was not an escape from Judaism to a "safer" faith, but, certainly, an embrace of both of them as only a woman like Edith Stein could do.

The years within the cloistered walls of Carmel in Cologne, oddly enough, brought Edith Stein closer to the world. Jewish friends and others who had heard of her, terrified and about to flee Germany, came to her and went away consoled and strengthened for the journey ahead. Her own study and writing burgeoned in a new direction. She continued her strong advocacy of the role of women but she also began to write about mysticism in a new and exciting way: not as an esoteric phenomenon available only to the chosen, but as everyone's journey beyond the realm of the senses in search of the ineffable God. God was for all, not a select few. And Edith Stein was revealing him in a simple and accessible way.

Kristallnacht has such a beautiful sound. Yet in the flash of a moment its meaning became horrid beyond words. In the night of November 8, 1938, Nazi S.S. troopers drove Jews from their homes with clubs, demolished or appropriated their businesses, desecrated and burned their synagogues. Their lives as members of German society were destroyed in that single night, the shattering of their temple windows an ominous sign that whatever National Socialism chose to do with them or to them was now sanctioned.

Edith Stein knew that with this brazen act of organized hate, her mere presence at the convent in Cologne made it more dangerous for the other nuns. She was the only Jew. She may have seen her destiny clearly, but she was not about to involve anyone else. She decided to go to the Carmelites at Echt, in Holland. But she sensed that it was just a matter of time before she would be asked to make her stand before the Nazi onslaught.

While the Catholic Church in other occupied countries tried in various ways to accommodate and placate the Nazis—even after the deportation of Jews began— the Dutch Church stood firm. A letter, harshly critical of the regime, was read from every pulpit in Holland on a July Sunday morning in 1942. Within two weeks, the Nazis responded with a calculated act that was intended to dampen any future meddling. Because of the Church's intransigence, all Catholics who were converted Jews were to be deported immediately.

The last days and hours of Edith Stein's life were

marked neither by any heroic act—she saved no one
from their fate—nor by any inspired words to soften the
hearts of her captors. Survivors remember her mostly as
being silent, and calm. She tended abandoned children,
washed clothes, comforted mothers insane with grief.
She prayed, alone, and with those who would join her.

It is a strange irony that Edith Stein was sent to
Auschwitz not only because she was a Jew, but a
Catholic Jew. And once there, amidst the panic and ter-
ror, the wailing of thousands of men and women about
to die, she walked among the victims of hate and
brought them the love she had found after such a long
search herself. It was all she could give. Condemned by
a soulless regime, the prisoners of Auschwitz with Edith
Stein at least had one comfort—the comfort of knowing, in a world that had treated them with such cruelty
and injustice, that someone cared.

She said it often, that love was stronger than hate,
and in those fetid boxcars bound for Auschwitz, in the
wretched quarters where the doomed were jammed, on
the very path to the gas chambers, Edith Stein proved it
was so.

After that horrible war ended and the nuns returned
to their ravaged convent at Echt, they found among
Edith Stein's papers this jotting, a meditation that sums
up her courage and the spiritual force that moved her:

> Do you want to be totally united to the Cruci-
> fied? If you are serious about this, you will be pre-
> sent, by the power of His cross, at every front, at
> every place of sorrow, bringing to those who suffer
> comfort, healing and salvation.

Herbstrith, Waltraud, *Edith Stein: A Biography,* trans. by Fr. Bernard Bonowitz, OCSO, Harper & Row, San Francisco, CA, 1985.